PROFIT

THROUGH THE

POST

ALISON CORK

PROFIT
THROUGH THE
POST

How to set up
and run a successful
Mail Order Business

PIATKUS

First published in Great Britain in 1994 by
Judy Piatkus (Publishers) Ltd of
5 Windmill Street, London W1P 1HF

The moral right of the author has been asserted

*A catalogue record for this book is available
from the British Library*

ISBN 0–7499 1313 4

Designed by Chris Warner
Edited by Carol Franklin

Set in 11/13pt Plantin by
Phoenix Photosetting, Chatham, Kent

Printed and bound in Great Britain by
Mackays of Chatham PLC, Chatham, Kent

For Mum, Dad and Christopher

ACKNOWLEDGEMENTS

To JG

also Ann Ahern, Reuben Ash, John Beale and Past Times, Gordon Bishop, Simon Cleaver and RDP, Derek Cottey and MOPS, The Data Protection Registrar, Patrick O'Dee and the ASA, Anne Fanning and Wyvern Crest Ltd, Roger Fowler, Anthony Gibson, Jeremy Isaac, Ian Jones and Tolson Messenger Ltd, David Kerley and Unwins Seeds Ltd, Michelle Kershaw and Lakeland Plastics Ltd, Howard Lewis and Hughes Allen, The Littlewoods Organisation Ltd, S.E. Marshall & Co. Ltd, Roger Neuman, The Observer Ltd, Lunn Poly, Melvin Powers and the Wilshire Book Company, Jayne Readman and The Public Relations Business, Jill and David Redbourn Miller and The Tin Pot Company, Rollexa Ltd, Bob Shannon, Christopher Tracy, Nina Webley, Steve White, Jonathan Willis, John Wilson and Weavers Press, Wesley Wood and The Writing School, variously for kind advice, helpful comment and permission to reproduce extracts from their work. Special thanks to my editor, Gill Cormode.

The author and publishers would like to thank the following people and organisations for kindly allowing them to reproduce their advertisements and logos in this book.

(p. 8) Paula Brooke; (p. 9) Melvin Powers; (p. 11) The Littlewoods Organisation Ltd; (pp. 33 & 169) Wesley Wood; (p. 82) The Advertising Standards Authority; (p. 89) MOPS; (p. 94) Data Protection Registrar; (pp. 105 & 134) John Wilson; (p. 114) Roger Neuman; (p. 116) Jonathan Willis; (pp. 121 & 126) The Observer Ltd; (p. 122) Carnell Ltd; (pp. 124, 210 & 211) S.E. Marshall & Co. Ltd; (p. 137) The Tin Pot Company; (pp. 212, 213 & 214) Lakeland Plastics Ltd; (p. 224) Bernard Price and Rollexa Ltd.

CONTENTS

INTRODUCTION

I N THE SPRING OF 1990 Carnell Ltd was in its infancy. Today it is a multi-million pound mail order publishing company, built up in just 3 years with a staff of only 5. And, just for the record, not one of us has had any formal business training. You might argue that we have simply been lucky with our products or part of a buoyant economy. But luck doesn't build a thriving business in the midst of the worst recession since the 1930s. The fact is that success in such a short time is something to be proud of, whichever way you care to look at it.

Part of our success lies in the nature of mail order itself and this is one of the reasons I recommend it as a form of trading; mail order is unique – it can be low risk, you can be small yet sell nationwide and, best of all, it is immediate. Having read this book you could be in business within a few weeks. Not only that, but you will also get feedback within days of running your first advertisement. Some people have to invest tens of thousands of pounds in a new business and wait years for an accurate readout, often to be told that they are not going to make it. The restaurant and retail trades are notorious for this.

You can, however, have proper control over your business. At worst, you may run a few ads that flop and decide that mail order is not for you. At best, your mail order business will develop slowly but surely, complementing your current business/lifestyle whilst generating welcome extra profits. Your only decision then will be whether to continue in a part-time capacity or develop the enterprise further. It's a choice that lots of people would give their eye teeth for, and it could be yours to make.

This book has been written for everyone who wishes to start trading by mail order, whether at home or as an extension of an established company. Over the next 12 chapters you will see why mail order is one of the most exciting and low risk opportunities of today. You will discover how to choose a suitable product (or assess one you already have) and set up a profitable enterprise – including all the secrets I have learnt about the mail order world! The book starts with a brief detour through the history and development of mail order, and goes on to deal with the practicalities of starting up and managing the growth that follows.

There are many books on the subject of mail order and in true entrepreneurial spirit they are always wildly enthusiastic and often over optimistic. In any business venture you should remember that you can lose, as well as make, money. In this book I have concentrated on the day-to-day practicalities of setting up so that you know realistically what to expect. The truth is that mail order *is* wonderful and exhilarating, and you *can* make a fortune. One or two of you, having read this book, might do just that, and others will do very nicely, thank you. But first you must focus on mastering the basics. Only then will the cheques follow.

Don't be discouraged if you have no previous business experience – lots of success stories started out that way! Of course, if you are already running a business you're one step ahead; but don't ignore the chapters on general business practice – they should still be relevant and useful. Either way, you won't find any unnecessary jargon, just simple, easy to understand instructions and lots of common sense. Best of all, you have absolutely nothing to lose by at least reading this book and you might just find that this is the chance you've been waiting for. So read on. . . .

Alison Cork
June 1993

1

WHAT IS
MAIL ORDER?

I N RETAILING TERMS, mail order is very much
the 'new kid on the block'. Shopkeepers have existed
in some shape or form for thousands of years, but mail
order came into being as recently as the nineteenth century.
Having said that, it has very quickly established a foothold in
retailing and emerged as a major growth area in the twentieth
century. But what exactly is mail order, how did it begin, in
what ways does it differ from other methods of selling and why
has it become a retailing phenomenon?

A BRIEF DEFINITION OF
THE MAIL ORDER BUSINESS

Mail order is just one aspect of a much larger phenomenon
called direct marketing, which has been defined by the DMMA
(Direct Mail/Marketing Association of America) as: 'The total
of activities by which products or services are offered to market
segments in one or more media for informational purposes or to
solicit a direct response from a present or prospective customer
or contributor by mail, telephone or other access.'

In plain English, direct marketing is all about using a variety of methods – newspapers, magazines, mail order catalogues, direct mail (i.e. mail addressed to you personally), radio, television and telephone all with the aim of either selling direct to the customer, getting enquiries or, occasionally, just generating awareness of a product.

The common aim of most direct marketing methods is the attempt to target the customer and to create a direct response from them (often via specially designed response mechanisms), and one which is both quantifiable and cost-effective. Direct marketing is a wonderfully exact medium, which enables both costs and sales to be measured precisely, and with much greater speed than one could measure the effect of a general and unfocused advertising campaign. If proof were needed of its success, the UK direct marketing industry is now worth over £12 billion a year (source: Direct Mail Information Service), and the volume of consumer direct mail doubled between 1983 and 1991 from 1 to 2 billion items (source: Royal Mail).

Where does mail order fit in?

Mail order is a significant subsection of the direct marketing industry. A recent Mintel report ('Home Shopping Specialists') stated that in 1992 '58 per cent of women and 48 per cent of men had used mail order'.

Basically, mail order is a trading method that uses particular media – newspapers, magazines, catalogues and mailing pieces – to advertise and sell products direct to the reader/customer. Only two parties are ever involved (the seller and the buyer) and the purchase is usually made through the initial advertisement (rather than with follow-up literature), often by filling out a coupon and sending it off with payment. The only real difference between mail order and direct marketing is that mail order offers are always products, whereas the direct marketing industry sells both products and services.

This book will concentrate on newspaper and magazine advertising as a widely applicable and cost-effective means of starting out in mail order. Catalogues and mailing lists will be examined in the context of expanding your business.

Ten characteristics of mail order

Mail order has several distinctive features.

1. Although the transaction is a direct one between seller and buyer, the two parties rarely meet in person. Communication is by mail or on the telephone.

2. The customer is unable to see or touch the product before paying for it.

3. The seller tries to compensate for this by giving a detailed product description in the advertisement and by offering a full money-back guarantee on each item.

4. The seller usually receives payment before the product is delivered to the customer.

5. The strength of the advertising copy is all-important. It has to be powerful enough to take the place of the tangible product. At its best, it can be even more effective than actually handling the item.

6. Originality is not necessarily the key to success. If the product is not being sold by mail order, it is either totally new and possibly a real winner, or, more probably, has already been tried without success. Most mail order traders look at what works elsewhere and follow that lead.

7. The choice of product available through mail order is vast but is often limited by its suitability as a postal item – size, shape, weight, fragility and perishability all need to be considered.

8. Most mail order items are classed as luxury goods, i.e. not a prerequisite of everyday life.

9. The effectiveness of a mail order campaign can be measured almost immediately. You can gauge the success of an ad within a few days, simply by looking at how many orders have come in. Your personal opinion is actually not very relevant – the volume of mail is the most honest and accurate indicator of product success/failure.

10. The real profit in mail order comes not just from the initial advertisement response but from building an ongoing customer relationship and selling to those people again. It is this element of long-term profitability that lies behind most mail order successes.

Finally, mail order is one of the few businesses that can be started part-time, with no previous experience, needing low overheads and with you exercising strict control over the financial risk. It can also be run alongside an existing business with the minimum of disruption. Mail order is unique and, like most good ideas, was developed in response to a gap in the market place.

MAIL ORDER ORIGINS: AMERICAN STYLE

Mail order is very much an American invention and if we look back to nineteenth century rural America it is easy to see why. At that time vast expanses of land were occupied by small, scattered farming communities, so isolated and inaccessible that all provisions had to be bought from local suppliers. Predictably, the range of goods was not only limited but also expensive. Result – the poor farmer had little choice but to either pay up or go without! Needless to say this became unpopular and gave birth to the demand, albeit unfocused at that stage, for alternative sources of supply.

The nineteenth century

At the same time the 1860s saw the rapid development of the postal system and thus the first attempts by manufacturers to offer their products through the mail. To begin with, manufacturers placed advertisements in local papers to encourage the reader to purchase from their local retail outlet. But so many people wrote in saying that the local outlet either didn't stock an item or was too far away that the manufacturer had to accommodate the customer by mailing the product directly to them. This became so lucrative that many manufacturers decided to alter the ads, giving more information about the product and soliciting the order direct from the ad itself. They also put in a money-back guarantee of satisfaction. And mail order was born!

The first recorded 'father' of mail order was E. C. Allen of Augusta, Maine, in about 1870. At the same time Montgomery Ward of Chicago, Illinois, used his knowledge as an ex-salesman to set up a mail order catalogue. But perhaps the most spectacular success of the nineteenth century was the famous Sears Roebuck operation, built out of a collaboration between Mr Sears (originally a watch salesman), Mr Roebuck and Mr Rosenwald. Together they developed a mail order company which not only prospered, but has lasted over a hundred years. In 1902 Sears Roebuck achieved sales of $50,000,000. At its height, the Sears Roebuck catalogue was second only to the Bible as the most popular book in the world!

The twentieth century

Mail order giants of twentieth-century America have included Robert Collier, who went from earning $25 a week as a lowly employee to building a business which at one point took $1 million worth of orders for a single book in less than six months; Joe Cossman, who became a multi-millionaire by selling, among other things, fly poison and toy soldiers by mail order; Joe Karbo, who went from the brink of bankruptcy in the 1960s to multi-millionaire status in the 1970s. How? He wrote a book called *The Lazy Man's Way to Riches* and sold over a million copies (see page 8); Len and Rick Hornick, who started with what was just a hobby and ended up with a multi-million dollar business (selling decoy ducks!); and Melvin Powers, a once unsuccessful author who took matters into his own hands, advertised his unpublished book and proceeded to build up a mail order business selling over 100,000 books every month (see page 9).

The Lazy Man's Way to Riches

'Most People Are Too Busy Earning a Living to Make Any Money'

I used to work hard. The 18-hour days. The 7-day weeks.

But I didn't start making big money until I did less—a lot less.

For example, this ad took about 2 hours to write. With a little luck, it should earn me 50, maybe a hundred thousand dollars.

What's more, I'm going to ask you to send me 10 dollars for something that'll cost me no more than 50 cents. And I'll try to make it so irresistible that you'd be a darned fool not to do it.

After all, why should you care if I make $9.50 profit if I can show you how to make a lot more?

What if I'm so sure that you will make money my Lazy Man's Way that I'll make you a most unusual guarantee?

And here it is: I won't even cash your check or money order for 31 days *after* I've sent you my material.

That'll give you plenty of time to get it, look it over, try it out.

If you don't agree that it's worth at *least* a hundred times what you invested, send it back. Your uncashed check or money order will be put in the return mail.

The only reason I won't send it to you and bill you or send it C.O.D. is because both these methods involve more time and money.

And I'm already going to give you the biggest bargain of your life.

Because I'm going to tell you what it took me 11 years to perfect: How to make money the Lazy Man's Way.

O.K.—now I have to brag a little. I don't mind it. And it's necessary—to prove that sending me the 10 dollars . . . which I'll keep "in escrow" until you're satisfied . . . is the smartest thing you ever did.

I live in a home that's worth $250,000. I know it is, because I turned down an offer for that much. My mortgage is less than half that, and the only reason I haven't paid it off is because my Tax Accountant says I'd be an idiot.

My "office," about a mile and a half from my home, is right on the beach. My view is so breathtaking that most people comment that they don't see how I get any work done. But I do enough. About 6 hours a day, 8 or 9 months a year.

The rest of the time we spend at our mountain "cabin." I paid $30,000 for it—cash.

I have 2 boats and a Cadillac. All paid for.

We have stocks, bonds, investments, cash in the bank. But the most important thing I have is priceless: time with my family.

And I'll show you just how I did it—the Lazy Man's Way—a secret that I've shared with just a few friends 'till now.

It doesn't require "education." I'm a high school graduate.

It doesn't require "capital." When I started out, I was so deep in debt that a lawyer friend advised bankruptcy as the only way out. He was wrong. We paid off our debts, and outside of the mortgage, don't owe a cent to any man.

It doesn't require "luck." I've had more than my share, but I'm not promising you that you'll make as much money as I have. And you may do better; I personally know one man who took these same principles, worked hard, and made 11 million dollars in 8 years. But money isn't everything.

It doesn't require "talent." Just enough brains to know what to look for. And I'll tell you that.

It doesn't require "youth." One woman I worked with is over 70. She's travelled the world over, making all the money she needs, doing only what I taught her.

It doesn't require "experience." A widow in Chicago has been averaging $25,000 a

" . . . I didn't have a job and I was worse than broke. I owed more than $50,000 and my only assets were my wife and 8 children. We were renting an old house in a decaying neighborhood, driving a 5-year old car that was falling apart, and had maybe a couple of hundred dollars in the bank.

Within one month, after using the principles of the Lazy Man's Way to Riches, things started to change — to put it mildly.

- We worked out a plan we could afford to pay off our debts — and stopped our creditors from hounding us.
- We were driving a brand-new Thunderbird that a car dealer had given to us!
- Our bank account had multiplied tenfold!
- All within the first 30 days!

And today . . .

- I live in a home that's worth over $250,000.
- I own my "office". It's about a mile and a half from my home and is right on the beach.
- I own a lakefront "cabin" in Washington. (That's where we spend the whole summer — loafing, fishing, swimming and sailing.)
- I own two oceanfront condominiums. One is on a sunny beach in Mexico and one is snuggled right on the best beach of the best island in Hawaii.
- I have two boats and a Cadillac. All paid for.
- I have a net worth of over a Million Dollars. But I still don't have a job . . ."

year for the past 5 years, using my methods.

What *does* it require? Belief. Enough to take a chance. Enough to absorb what I'll send you. Enough to put the principles into action. If you do just that—nothing more, nothing less—the results will be hard to believe. Remember—I guarantee it.

You don't have to give up your job. But you may soon be making so much money that you'll be able to. Once again—I guarantee it.

The wisest man I ever knew told me something I never forgot: "Most people are too busy earning a living to make any money."

Don't take as long as I did to find out he was right.

Here are some comments from other people. I'm sure that, like you, they didn't believe me either. Guess they figured that, since I wasn't going to deposit their check for 31 days, they had nothing to lose.

They were right. And *here's what they gained:*

$260,000 in eleven months

"Two years ago, I mailed you ten dollars in sheer desperation for a better life . . . One year ago, just out of the blue sky, a man called and offered me a partnership . . . I grossed over $260,000 cash business in eleven months. You are a God sent miracle to me."

B. F., Pascagoula, Miss.

Made $16,901.92 first time out

"The third day I applied myself totally to what you had shown me. I made $16,901.92. That's great results for my first time out."

J. J. M., Watertown, N.Y.

I'm a half-millionaire'

"Thanks to your method, I'm a half-millionaire . . . would you believe last year at this time I was a slave working for peanuts?"

G. C., Toronto, Canada

$7,000 in five days

"Last Monday I used what I learned on page 83 to make $7,000. It took me all week to do it, but that's not bad for five day's work."

M. D., Topeka, Kansas

Can't knock success

"I can't believe how successful I have become . . . Three months ago, I was a telephone order taker for a fastener company in Chicago, Illinois. I was driving a beat-up 1959 Rambler and had about

$600 in my savings account. Today, I am the outside salesman for the same fastener company. I'm driving a company car . . . I am sitting in my own office and have about $3,000 in my savings account."

G. M., Des Plaines, Ill.

I know you're skeptical. After all, what I'm saying is probably contrary to what you've heard from your friends, your family, your teachers and maybe everyone else you know. I can only ask you one question.

How many of them are millionaires?

A month from today, you can be nothing more than 30 days older — or you can be on your way to getting rich. You decide.

Joe Karbo's famous advertisement.

HOW I MADE $1,000,000 IN MAIL ORDER

tells how

YOU CAN MAKE $1,000,000 IN MAIL ORDER

WHAT THIS BOOK CAN DO FOR YOU

If you want to break out of the old rut—start your own business with little or no capital necessary—and be your own boss at last—mail order is the greatest business opportunity that can do this for you.

In this book I will show you how to think up a mail order product and test it inexpensively (following the advertising system given in these pages), produce it and market it. Starting with just one product, and working in your spare time or just on weekends, it is actually possible to bring in several thousand dollars a day in cash-in-advance orders!

That is what makes mail order the fastest-growing and most profit-making business in the world today. This book will show you how to go about it, from getting the first idea right on through to establishing an entire line of successful merchandise for your own mail order business.

I started out using the kitchen table as a desk and working on weekends while keeping my regular nine-to-five job. Today I own the office building in which I work and sit behind a $1,000 desk.

In these pages you'll discover how with common sense, imagination, and perseverance you can do the same, building a business with unlimited potential and adventure.

E. JOSEPH COSSMAN

"I have been in the mail order business for 25 years and during this time I have read every book I could find on the subject. In my opinion, Joe Cossman's book, **How I Made $1,000,000 In Mail Order**, is one of the best mail order books ever written."

Melvin Powers

Please send your order to:
Melvin Powers
12015 Sherman Road, North Hollywood, California 91605

MAIL NO-RISK TRIAL COUPON TODAY!

Gentlemen: Send me a copy of HOW I MADE $1,000,000 IN MAIL ORDER by E. Joseph Cossman. Price $11.00 postpaid.

I will use this book for 30 days entirely at your risk. If I am not thoroughly pleased, I will simply return this book for a full refund.

Enclosed is my check ☐ cash ☐ money order ☐ for $11.00

Name _____
(Please print)

Address _____

City _____ Zone _____ State _____

Money-spinning copy from Melvin Powers.

Mail order has become a fully established part of the American dream. People love to use it and fortunes are made from it. Until a few years ago the story was a very different one in the UK, but things are now changing . . .

HOW MAIL ORDER HAS COME OF AGE IN THE UK

In the UK we have been somewhat slower to embrace mail order, mainly because our country is quite compact and, relatively speaking, more densely populated; most of us are within easy reach of the shops and in any case most have access to a car or public transport.

The beginnings . . .

The first signs of the industry were back in the 1930s when people such as Littlewoods, Freemans and Grattans used a network of agents to sell catalogue items, mainly to those of a lower income bracket. The first Littlewoods catalogue was published in May 1932 (see page 11). It had 168 pages (the 1992 catalogue had 1,068 pages) and included items such as Axminster rugs, writing desks, 'Afternoon Frocks, Housemaid's' and 'dinner wagons'.

It paved the way for the modern home shopping industry, offering value for money and a full guarantee on all items ordered. John Moores, founder of Littlewoods, recalled the emphasis on quality and value: 'We examined everything carefully. I remember sitting and stripping off the leather sole of a shoe with my penknife, to make sure it actually did have triple soles, as advertised.' Today, mail order items are no longer sold just through catalogues and, unlike the 1930s, are now bought by people of all socio-economic categories; Queen

A page from an early Littlewoods mail order catalogue.

Noor of Jordan recently said that she does a lot of shopping this way!

Modern day mail order

Mail order now comes in all shapes and forms.

1. Retail stores now offer a mail order service – shops such as Selfridges, Marks & Spencer, Next and Laura Ashley immediately spring to mind.
2. Newspapers and especially the Sunday colour supplements are littered with adverts from both large and small mail order companies selling clothes, household gadgets, gardening equipment, books, health and beauty products, fitness aids etc.
3. The leaflets that come with the newspapers – tempting offers for the ultimate executive toy, replica items from British history, toys, games, and sometimes quite expensive items of porcelain, jewellery and art.
4. Last, but not least, there is an absolute plethora of clothes catalogues on the market – huge tomes that rival the telephone directory in size and weight.

When you come to think about it, mail order is all around you and expanding by leaps and bounds. The reasons for this are quite easily identifiable, as follows.

An increase in disposable income

In broad terms and compared to the first half of the twentieth century, people now have more money than ever to spend on non-essential items. This disposable income is the mainstay of mail order activity. However much you may desire a limited edition teddy bear, it cannot be classed as an essential requirement for life and nor are the majority of mail order products.

Increased income levels have undoubtedly contributed to the development of the mail order industry and, although you will see later that most people can be persuaded to buy through the post, the majority are those from a higher income bracket. Consequently, mail order now has a somewhat more sophisticated image and is no longer associated with people wishing to buy 'on tick'. Companies such as Racing Green have proved that people are happy to pay for quality mail order items, in this case smart, well made clothes.

Changes in leisure patterns

This phenomenon has greatly affected mail order. More and more women are now going out to work and consequently have less time to shop. As a result, what leisure time they and their partners do have is much more precious. While it is true that some people do consider shopping a leisure activity (yes, really!), most think of it as a chore and the time-saving aspect of mail order buying has scored highly. Mail order companies have tried to turn this to their advantage by emphasising the 'luxury of shopping from your armchair'.

Consumer credit

This has had as startling an effect upon mail order as it has upon high street shopping. The use of credit cards not only makes it easier to sell by mail but also gives the customer greater flexibility as to when they have to pay for the item. For the same reason, it encourages people to spend more than they might otherwise do, knowing that repayments can be spread over a period of time.

The increasing expense of 'on the road' salespeople

The average person's salary, car, petrol, insurance, allowances, commission and administration can cost their company over £43,000 a year (source: The Reward Group, 1992/3 figure). That amount of money can generate considerably greater profit when spent on a mail order advertising budget – partly because you can exercise much greater control over an advertising budget than you can over a person. Even when it doesn't actually replace the salesperson, mail order can still be used in tandem, principally to locate and confirm leads. It can be a very cost-effective medium.

From the shopkeeper's point of view, high property prices, large overheads and difficulties finding and keeping good staff makes mail order an attractive alternative for them also. For a start, they no longer need smart, high visibility premises, and can reduce their rent and rate charges at the same time. A mail order operator's shop-window is not their office, but their advertisement, as we shall see later on.

The development and sophistication of computer systems

This has helped mail order by speeding up and improving customer service. Details held on computer can be recalled at the touch of a button, telling you who the customer is, where they live, what they ordered, how they paid and when the order was dispatched. This becomes very important when you want to expand the business; one of the best ways to do so is to go back, analyse your customer information and try to sell to these people a second time. They are your strongest leads – after all, they have bought from you once before!

All these factors explain why mail order has become a viable alternative to shop sales from the businessperson's point of view, but why does the customer like mail order?

WHO BUYS MAIL ORDER AND WHY?

Understanding the motivation of your mail order customer is most important. It will give you all the clues as to what you should and shouldn't sell by mail. The question of choosing a product will be examined in more detail in Chapter 3, but in the mean time you should get into the habit of seeing things from the customers' point of view. Your job is to satisfy their needs and demands. In return they will make you a profit; they are certainly not going to spend money indulging your whims if you choose to sell a product for the wrong reasons; always look first at what people want and then try to fill that gap.

The attractions of mail order

People use mail order for quite varied reasons.

Convenience

This is probably the single, most important benefit to the mail order customer. The Mintel report mentioned above also stated that one in three adults like the fact that mail order allows them to look and choose in the comfort of their own home. While mail order certainly hasn't taken the place of retail shopping and probably never will, it does two crucial things.

- It offers products not available locally to the customer – thus allowing the person living in Wales to buy a product from London just by walking to the post-box.
- It meets the current consumer demand for greater ease and convenience when spending money. Crowded shops, unhelpful staff, expensive or non-existent parking facilities and endless queues all fuel this demand. These days the customer has higher expectations of comfort and service – which is actually no bad thing.

The convenience factor has given rise to whole new sales concepts. When the Wyvern Business Library started selling business books by mail order over 13 years ago, they were also starting a new tradition. Previously, business books could only be bought through bookshops, but most businesspeople simply didn't have the time to go to the shops and browse. When they did, it was for pleasure and not for business. Wyvern very specifically used mail order to address businesspeople at their place of work, probably just when they realised their need for a problem-solving book. Despite the fact that bookshops have greatly improved their business book departments, Wyvern still does a roaring trade, simply because they can deliver a good selection of titles straight to the businessperson's desk.

Novelty

Many successful mail order companies offer items not to be found in retail outlets (or they are, but badly marketed!). This can either be something purely practical, i.e. a particular item exclusive to the supplier, but is more often a novelty item and something desired by the customer because the neighbours haven't got it! Don't underestimate this aspect of mail order; a colleague of mine runs a successful mail order business selling rare varieties of flower and vegetable seeds. Many of his customers are responding purely to what I call the 'Harvest Festival syndrome' – the desire to grow something bigger, better and more unusual than everyone else in the street. My friend has simply recognised and exploited this gap in the market.

Price and choice advantage

Low overheads mean that items bought through mail order can be somewhat cheaper than their retail counterparts; even if you had to pay rent for your office space and were not working from home, it is unlikely that this would cost you as much as the rent on a high street retail position, all of which has to be reflected in your prices. Mail order items aren't always cheaper however; if they have a novelty value or are exclusive to one supplier, they may well carry a premium. One of your pricing considerations should always be 'what the market will bear', i.e. what people are prepared to pay (see Chapter 4).

Also, any price advantage to the customer can either be a reality or just their perception; if, for example, you were offering an item for £10.95 + £2 postage and packaging, the real cost to the customer is obviously £12.95. Strangely enough though, the customer concentrates on the amount of £10.95, forgetting the fact that p&p has to be added, and that they wouldn't pay p&p if they bought the item in a shop! You will find throughout this book that psychology plays a very important part in mail order.

Special interest items

These are often bought through the post, especially if unavailable locally; stamps, coins, gardening items, 'self-improvement' material, memorabilia and miniatures all sell well by mail order. Again, this is a case of the mail order supplier identifying a demand and the customer responding to it. Moreover, most collectors will pay a premium for something of particular interest to them. An American colleague of mine brings out a solid gold miniature coin commemorating John Kennedy's assassination, each year on his anniversary. It never fails to sell. People either buy because they are coin collectors, or they want it as a gift, as a possible investment or simply because of the American fascination with the Kennedy family. 'Special interest' items are always in demand.

Fun, excitement and, above all, impulse

These are important mail order motivations. People love receiving packages and parcels through the post, especially if they have forgotten what they ordered (as they often do!) and it comes as a complete surprise. Impulse is a very important factor and one which must be properly understood.

Most mail order companies identify a need/demand and set about satisfying it, i.e. they are students of markets first, then of products and this is the normal way to succeed. But it is also true that a number of your mail order customers will be impulse buyers. Here it is up to you to entice the customer on the strength of your advertising copy. This time you have chosen the product and your job is to make the reader buy, even though they certainly didn't set out that morning with the intention of making a purchase. This is the really exciting part of mail order – the psychological warfare! Imagine the thrill of being able to persuade people to send you money for one of your products, without even meeting them!

Impulse items are often gadgets or gifts and that is why they are particularly strong in the run up to Christmas when everyone is desperate to find an unusual present. Some mail order catalogues, particularly those that come with Sunday papers, are almost entirely composed of impulse goods. Hands up those of you who have succumbed to hi-tech water bottles, performance enhanced golf balls, expandable shoe racks or instant tooth whitener!

Loneliness and physical disability

Lastly, and on a more sober note, loneliness and physical disability play their part in the mail order world. It is very sad but undoubtedly true that people who are housebound, alone, unwell and often quite elderly use mail order not just as a convenience but also to guarantee a visit from the postman. It is a rather poor reflection upon the rest of us I'm afraid, but it is none the less something you should be aware of. Looking at it more positively, there is obviously a market for home aids and gadgets that might improve mobility and help towards a better quality of life. Some of the most enduring newspaper advertisements of recent years have been those for electric stair lifts, help alarms and bath grips.

Mail order is a fascinating, fast growing and psychologically complex field. The reasons why you should join the industry are much more transparent and the ease with which you can do so is one of mail order's greatest attractions . . .

2

WHY CHOOSE MAIL ORDER?

I N CHAPTER 1 we looked at the social, economic and technological reasons why mail order has taken off in the UK. But there is another side to the equation; however valid the factors which encourage an industry to emerge, there have to be sufficient numbers of people willing and able to work in that particular field in order to ensure its stability and future growth.

Mail order has succeeded partly because it doesn't put up great barriers to entry – academic, financial, practical or otherwise. You can either start from scratch or expand your existing business by offering the added facility of mail order sales. Either way, it is possible with mail order to monitor your progress on a daily basis and keep finances under control. Moreover, you can build the business at a pace to suit yourself. Mail order need only be a full-time commitment when you want it to be. Does this sound too good to be true? You will have to decide for yourself.

THE 'PERFECT' JOB

Mail order really does stand out as being quite unusual in the amount of flexibility and job satisfaction it can give. I can't think of many other opportunities that offer all of the following.

Flexibility as to where you work

For those of you with an existing business you need simply to set aside some space for the mail order operation, ideally a room or two. As a beginner to mail order and to business, you can (and should) start small and at home. It is easy enough to move on once the business grows – mail order is very much a moveable feast! In the meantime you have eliminated the expense and time previously taken in travelling, and can enjoy the comfort and convenience of working from home.

Moreover, working from a restricted space doesn't mean that your range of customers has to be limited in any way; mail order is one of the few trading methods by which a person can sell to almost anybody else in their country (even worldwide) – without actually leaving their office premises or their home!

Flexibility as to when you work

This applies more to those people who want to start up from home. It is where mail order really comes into its own by allowing you to balance work with other commitments. Whether you are already in paid employment and want to test your idea on a small scale before going full-time, or are not in paid work but with other responsibilities – a home, children etc. – mail order can fit in with your daily schedule. You are not relying upon anyone else's involvement, but simply reacting to advertisement response. You could therefore continue your daily routine around opening the post and sending out orders.

Even if you had a full-time job to start with, you could conceivably manage these tasks in the evening after work and send out the orders in the post next morning, albeit on a small scale. In the long term you can also take holidays, career breaks or maternity leave and not be disadvantaged when you return – you simply stop advertising your product and then start again when you are ready.

Flexibility as to how you grow

Again, you exercise complete control. You may have dreams of building an empire. You may just want basic financial independence. The beauty of mail order is that it can accommodate either ambition. Mail order can be very big. It can also be very small. But the principle upon which you trade remains the same: you test an advertisement until you find the proposition that works best. You then capitalise upon this success by running the same winning formula in other publications. You do not commit to several ads before you know which one works. In other words, you do not take unnecessary risks. How many other business opportunities allow you that control?

QUALIFICATIONS AND SKILLS NECESSARY TO START

In a word, *none!* Most businesses and jobs require an initial period of training or study; with mail order you can start with a basic knowledge of both the industry and business practice – and these areas are dealt with in this book in sufficient detail to allow you to get established. Mail order is a great leveller of people – age, sex, background and education count for very little. There are no tests, examinations or other requirements (apart from membership of one or two regulatory bodies – see Chapter 6). You can enter the world of mail order more quickly and easily than you can almost any other business; in fact, as soon as you have finished reading this book. But don't think that this means everyone who tries will succeed. If that were the case there would be many more than 20,000 millionaires in this country! To succeed you will have to demonstrate the following abilities.

Professionalism

Customer service is so important that I have devoted a whole chapter to it later on and this is where your professionalism will pay dividends. Don't bother to read any further if you are not prepared to be ethical, fair, prompt and courteous. Your business will only prosper if you can encourage loyalty and repeat orders from your customers. There is always going to be someone who believes that they can dash in, relieve the customer of their money, send out a shoddy product and offer no follow-up service. And you probably *can* do it once, but only once. People take a great leap of faith when they put their hard-earned money into the post. If you let them down they will feel foolish and then angry. At the very least they will never purchase from you again, and they may well take revenge by making an official complaint to one of the industry's governing bodies. It simply isn't worth it – so don't try!

Effort

Mail order may be a relatively straightforward business to get into, but, and there's always a but, your results will only ever be commensurate with the effort you put in. In this book you will find out how to find a mail order product, advertise it, keep the customer happy and expand upon your success. You will actually have to go out there and do it. Above all else you will have to show patience and concentration when advertising your product until the right wording and media are found; and thoroughness, because only accurate and regular record-keeping will show you where to advertise next.

Luck helps, but most of the time it is intelligent detective work which uncovers a winning product, and hard work which creates a successful advertising campaign.

Most important, you should know every part of your business. Even when you expand and employ others, make sure that you still know how to write ads, analyse results etc. Know how to tackle all the problems yourself. If you lose sight of the everyday, you will also lose control.

Realism

Having said the above, don't punish yourself if you fail to make money at the very first attempt. Of course, no one can afford to lose indefinitely, but you have to accept that for every few successful ads there will be one or two that fail. In my business, which is publishing and selling books by mail order, we run hundreds of ads each year, covering 20 or so new titles at any one time. If 7 lose money, 10 break even and 3 do very well, we reckon to be having a good year. Those three successes will cancel the losses on the other books and go on to make the overall company profit. So don't be too hard on yourself. Remember that any business is about luck as well as conscientious effort, and even the experts make mistakes. Melvin Powers once said: 'Don't expect success with every mail order campaign. It just doesn't happen, not even to the experts. If you have given your best effort to a mail order idea and it doesn't work, put your energy into the next project.'

Remember the above, otherwise you may unnecessarily cut short a promising career! Take comfort from the fact that even experienced mail order companies make mistakes; Lakeland Plastics have built up a wonderful business selling catering equipment. However, even they came a cropper with the Steak Thermometer, a gadget which was designed to gauge the 'doneness' of your steak. It simply wasn't the seller they had hoped it would be.

Creativity

Try to be flexible in the way that you think about and analyse your business. Always try to understand what your customer wants and work back from there. Be open-minded about new ideas and products. Above all, don't allow your thinking to be a limitation to the business. You may not want to *Win Friends and Influence People*, but six and a half million other people were sufficiently interested to buy Dale Carnegie's book. You may not suffer from baldness, but a certain advertisement for hair restorer appears almost daily in the national newspapers (which must mean that it is making money). I do not own a cat, but three million people in Great Britain do, and 55,000 of them bought a copy of our publication *How to Talk to Your Cat*. So be receptive to trends, fashions, needs and desires – even if they aren't yours!

Having said that, don't allow your creativity to intrude upon your analysis of advertisement results. Your personal opinion should not play a big part in assessing product performance. There you have to trust in the volume of mail. Unless there is a particular reason to doubt it (more about that in Chapter 11), your postbag will deliver all the answers. Personal opinion can often just distort the true picture. At the end of the day, your sales totals alone will highlight very clearly what is succeeding and what is not. You must not assume you know better.

RESOURCES REQUIRED

'I know of no business in the world that requires such a small investment to start, and yet holds the promise of such tremendous financial gains as mail order' (Joe Cossman). Mail order is remarkable in that it demands so few resources to get started. Most new businesses have at least four requirements, as follows.

Capital

Capital is one of the biggest barriers to people entering business. Mail order is different. Of course, you do need money to start in mail order, as in any business. You must also realise that any business can lose as well as make money. But the crucial difference with mail order is that you can limit your financial risk. The secret of mail order success is to be informed and cautious; you try one advertisement. If it works and makes money you run it again elsewhere. If it doesn't you decide how many times you are prepared to test new approaches. Apart from the costs of setting up and of the product itself, the most you can lose is the money on the first few ads (and only if they all fail outright), because after that you simply don't repeat that particular advertisement. You set a limit on how much money you are prepared to risk overall, and then call a halt if and when that point is reached.

Obviously there will be some immediate financial outlay and this has to be met out of your pocket. You will soon learn to be resourceful – ordering up the smallest quantity of product possible for a test, trying to get credit terms on the advertising and not splashing out on, for example, fancy stationery. But bear in mind too that if you are without a track record in business you could well be asked to pay for items in advance. You will therefore need to consider the following when estimating your initial investment:

- the cost of stock;
- office and administration costs;
- advertising and dispatch;
- miscellaneous – accountants/solicitors etc.

Each of these areas will be looked at in more detail later on in this book. But briefly, if you are starting from scratch you should allow a minimum of £5,000 to give yourself a fair chance of meeting all expenses (1993 figures). Roughly broken down, you will need £1,000 for stock, £1,000 for office and admin, £2,500 for advertising and dispatch, and £500 for accountants

etc. Any less than that and you haven't allowed for the unexpected. This is by necessity a generalisation. There are, of course,
people who have started and succeeded with only £1,000. But
they are exceptions to the rule. You should always aim to err on
the side of caution.

It is best not to borrow money if possible. It is far better to
risk your own than have the worry of losing and owing that
money to a friend or to the bank. Using your own money will
also focus your mind very clearly on how you spend! Have a
contingency plan as well; if the mail order business doesn't
work out you will need to get rid of stock; this could be done via
a market stall or through a wholesaler. Whichever you choose,
don't leave yourself exposed.

Once the very first ad is running you will have the benefit of
immediate cash flow because people have to send in their money
with the order. It is a very simple principle, but this is one of
mail order's most valuable characteristics. Very few other businesses get paid 'up front' and very many otherwise solid ideas
founder because money owed to the company arrives later than
money owing to creditors. Result – they go out of business. Of
course, good cash flow isn't enough in itself, you also have to be
making a profit (see Chapter 5). But it does help!

Equipment and premises

In the early days you will not need a computer or any special
machinery, just a room, a desk and a telephone (which can be
your existing domestic line if necessary). Compare that to a
shop which needs special decor, furniture, cash tills, counters,
storage etc., all of which have to comply with various official
regulations, costing even more in the process.

Employees

Unless you find a 'winner' straight away, which is unlikely, you
should be quite capable of managing alone until such time as
you wish to expand. Even then, you could subcontract to a ful-

filment house (see Chapter 9), so that the really time-consuming job is off your hands, leaving you free for the important task of analysing the results. A mail order company with a turnover of several million pounds a year can easily manage with only a handful of people on the payroll. All receipt and subsequent dispatch of orders can be done by other companies.

A large investment of time

With mail order you start on a small scale until your results suggest that you should go for it! Having said that, you may never want to. A lot of mail order people make just a few pounds each week – but over the year that equates to a holiday, some home improvements, or any number of small luxuries that improve the quality of their life. There is absolutely nothing wrong with that. Not everyone can or wants to be a Joe Karbo.

Even if you do want to expand further than that, your personal involvement could eventually be confined to choosing products and analysing results, the linch-pin of mail order. All fulfilment and administration can be done successfully by employees and subcontracted companies.

WHAT ARE YOUR CHANCES OF SUCCESS?

They are already good for all the reasons we have discussed in this chapter and are enhanced by the fact that you have the benefit of this book to guide you through the whole process. Even when you run advertisements that lose money, you can control the damage so that when you hit a winner, you can cover those losses and go on to make a profit. No other business allows you such freedom to test, modify and learn as you go along. No other business gives you this amount of control and such a great chance of success. But do remember that success can never be guaranteed. You must always be realistic about the possibility of losing money and progress cautiously at all times.

It is now time to move away from the theory of mail order and look at the practice, which is, after all, the main purpose of this book. If you can master the following five key steps you will stand a good chance of achieving mail order success. It is these areas that we shall now go on to explore:

- **choosing a winning product;**
- **writing ads that pull response;**
- **accurate and prompt fulfilment;**
- **analysing results accurately;**
- **following up with other products or services.**

3

FINDING THAT WINNING PRODUCT

T O QUOTE JOE KARBO, 'the best product is between your ears'. By this he meant that it is not so much what you sell as how you sell it; your imagination and flair in advertising an item is as important as the item itself. This is undoubtedly true, but there are certain qualities which every good mail order product should have, without which you are unlikely to succeed. There is no point in even thinking about setting up your office until you have a proper product to sell. You may already have something you want to offer by mail order. You may just want to trade by mail order but do not yet have a product. Either way, don't commit yourself to any item until you have compared it with the checklist given here. Above all else, don't think you can break the rules. Mail order is a science and assessing/pricing a product is pretty much like following a formula. Don't try to be clever – learn from the experiences of others.

THE 10 SECRET INGREDIENTS OF A MAIL ORDER PRODUCT

In a perfect world, every mail order product would possess the following 10 characteristics. It rarely happens, but you should aim for as many of them as possible.

1. There has to be a demand for it

If you follow only one piece of advice in this chapter, let it be this:

LEARN TO BE A STUDENT OF MARKETS.

Always look first at what people want and then find the product to satisfy the need. Never take on a product just because you have fallen in love with it. Learn to distance yourself from your personal likes and dislikes. Establish the demand and then set about supplying it. This can't be emphasised enough. It really is the fundamental key to a mail order product.

Richard Branson made his first fortune selling records through the post. He didn't just pluck the idea out of the air. He found out that people wanted the option of purchasing records by mail as well as in the shops. Joe Karbo made millions by selling *The Lazy Man's Way to Riches*. He realised the desire that lies in most people – to be wealthy – and simply wrote a book about how to achieve it. John Beale, managing director of Past Times, researched the American market in museum gifts, and subsequently launched a very successful gift catalogue in Great Britain, selling wonderful 'gifts inspired by the past'.

Look at what sells already

'But', you ask, 'how can I tell if there is a demand?' The most obvious way is to see what people are already buying, i.e. what is sold most frequently through mail order. I emphasize mail order, because what sells well through shops will not necessarily be a mail order winner unless it conforms to the other characteristics laid out here (take note if you already sell a product that you want to offer through the post). You can be sure that no mail order operator will consistently run ads that lose money – they couldn't afford to. It therefore follows that there must be a demand for a product that regularly appears in mail order advertisements.

By observing this you will know what sells without having to spend money trying to find out. You will also see where and even how you might advertise your product, simply by looking at what others do. Don't be discouraged by this approach or worry that you are copying other people. At the end of the day, you are in business to make money, not to take unnecessary risks. It is, moreover, a basic business principle: look at the breakfast cereal market – different companies all trying to capture the same audience with variations on the basic breakfast cereal. Look at any confectionery counter – endless brand names, all after the cocoa addicts among us, and all just variations of good old chocolate. New ideas are extremely rare in this world and you should begin by understanding that important fact.

The best form of market research you can do is buy the daily and weekend national papers on a regular basis. Make notes on any ad that appears more than once, where it appears and when. Start a file of these ads. As this file builds up, you will begin to get a picture of what type of product sells consistently well by mail order. If you were to keep this file over a period of years, you would also notice that the most successful products, for example diets, books on how to make money, and personalised goods, come back time and time again. It is a fascinating exercise and one you should do on a regular basis.

Be a creative copycat

These two examples of cereals and chocolate are important because they illustrate another point. You cannot literally copy someone else's product and advertising campaign. This is neither ethical, nor will it work – for two reasons.

- You do not have all the information that is available to your competitor, and may be making incorrect assumptions about the product and its profitability.
- You may be trying to break in on a market so dominated by a particular product that you just cannot wrench away the business. One of our most successful books was called *The Government Auction Handbook*. Our campaign became so huge that at any one time we had advertisements in almost every national newspaper, many of them full-page. Of course it spawned a small army of would-be imitators. But no one could afford to make anything like the impact we had created and their ads just fizzled out. People associated the book with us and nobody else. (See page 116.)

What you should do, however, is learn to be creative and give an old product a new twist. Think about how you can improve upon or vary what exists, and then tell people about these new aspects in your advertising. Your product doesn't have to be completely exclusive. But equally, if it is easily available else-where, by mail or in the shops, why should people buy it from you? Let's say you have noticed that children's clothes sell well. Now tell the customer about your new range that is resistant to most food stains! My company saw that tomato plants/seeds seemed to do very well through mail order; our American colleagues introduced us to something much more exciting than the common old tom – a giant version – and we had tremendous success selling the 'Miracle Bush Tomato'! (See opposite.) The need for creativity in mail order is no more apparent than here. Think about new angles.

What if I have an original product?
This is not to say that there aren't new products to be discovered. Every now and again someone comes up with a pro-duct so unique that it storms the market and creates its own

demand. The Black and Decker Workmate was one, as were
Rubik's Cubes, all those 'executive desk toys', skateboards, the
mechanical 'bag of laughs', the 'pet rock' and the anti-theft
steering lock. If you think you have found something new, ask
yourself if it possesses characteristics 2 to 10, as set out below.
In addition, will it be easy for you to produce or acquire? There
is no point in offering something you then cannot fulfil because
your production capacity is insufficient or your supplier lets
you down. And lastly, can you afford to run a fast and
aggressive campaign, before the copycats get you?

2. It should have mass appeal

It is common sense that your product should appeal to as many
people as possible. The advertising is going to cost you the same
regardless, so you should always aim for the maximum audience. A truly great mail order product will transcend barriers of
age, race, sex, class and religion. It will appeal to our basic
human desires: wealth, health, beauty, success and power.
Successful mail order products usually touch upon one or more
of these areas.

Do you remember the Charles Atlas ads? For years these
exercise courses were a huge seller. They didn't just promise
fitness, they implied that every 7-stone weakling could become
attractive, popular and, by association, successful and wealthy.
No more sand in his face! Corny maybe, but also a multi-million
pound industry, since dieting and physical fitness is one of the
great obsessions of our time. Finding a product with mass
appeal is one of the fundamental ways to ensure success.

An exception to the rule . . .
However, you can also make a virtue out of a product with
specialist appeal. You may have an item which attracts a specific
sex or age group, e.g. a beauty product for women or a piece of
sports kit for the soccer-mad youngster. Equally you may have
something for the enthusiast or collector, e.g. stamps, militaria,
fishing products. Cornering a specialist market can have quite

an impact in terms of sales volume. If you can find the relevant niche magazine, e.g. one for coin collectors, it is likely that a high proportion of them will be interested in your special edition gold coin. Because you have targeted your audience so carefully you should get a high level of response from a relatively small circulation paper/magazine. Ultimately you may do just as well as if you had taken a more general product and attempted to sell it to the mass market, appealing to some and not to others.

Either way, whether your product has mass or specialist appeal, it must be one that you can describe clearly and convincingly. A large part of your success will depend upon your advertisement, so make sure that your product can be presented enticingly on paper.

3. There must be a sufficient profit margin

In Chapter 4 the subject of analysing product costs will be looked at in more detail, but the general rule is that you need to charge the customer at least three times the cost price of the product to ensure a satisfactory profit margin, and five times is preferable. Pay particular attention to this if you are trying to extend shop sales to include mail order. Many shop goods cannot achieve this cost/sales price ratio. It is vital that you offer only those products that do. Some mail order goods have much higher margins; books are an example, where ratios of up to 10:1 can be achieved! You will also find that most 'cash off the page' products sell for between £5 and £50, with the majority over £10.

4. It must be suitable as a postal item

Generally speaking, your product will have to survive an often undignified journey through the post. It should therefore be durable, preferably quite light, not too bulky, non-fragile and

non-perishable. Of course, there are always exceptions to the
rule: the Grattan catalogue actually managed to sell 1,000
Grandfather clocks through the mail! The American Joe Cossman apparently sold mail order ant farms and even toy shrun-
ken heads! The list of unlikely products is a long one. But for
the sake of convenience and from a beginner's point of view,
you should opt for more manageable items.

5. Choose a product you like and know about

This may seem a strange comment, but it is actually quite difficult to work with and promote a product with which you aren't
familiar. Your prejudice or ignorance will almost certainly
show in the advertising copy, whether you realise it or not. If
you were to analyse the most successful mail order advertisements you would find that they were almost always written
by people who knew their product. Don't be tempted by an
item just because it appears to be very profitable. Remember
that you have to write the advertisement.

If something gives you pleasure it will be easier to sell and
also more fun. Say you have a particular passion for gardens and
plants; you would probably feel much more convincing about
selling a gardening book than one on toy soldiers. However,
don't confuse this issue with identifying your markets. If
people want toy soldiers then you would be foolish to deny
them. But, wherever possible, try to match the demand with
something for which you feel an affinity.

6. A product which is readily available

It is illegal to offer an item by mail order if you don't have sufficient supplies to satisfy the expected response. (See Part B14(1)
and (2) of the British Code of Advertising Practice.) This stock
must be under your control, i.e. paid for and on your premises.
You cannot 'forward trade', i.e. wait for the advertisement

response and then order up the necessary quantity. There are a few exceptions to this rule:

- if your product is a bespoke item;
- if the product is advertised as being delivered in stages;
- if you are selling plants;
- if you manufacture the goods on your premises and have the raw materials to hand.

Quite apart from this legal aspect, what would you do if your supplier chose to let you down at the wrong moment? Be aware that the advertising and mail order authorities are within their rights to ask you at any given time to prove that you have sufficient stock available. There is no point in shooting yourself in the foot and choosing an item for which there is only an erratic supply.

7. It should be a repeat item

If at all possible you want your item to have a repeat purchase factor. Your real money will be made from those who order the same item again, because the second time around you have effectively cut out the major expense of advertising. Consequently, the profit margin on these items shoots up. It might be that your product has a limited lifespan, e.g. custom-made fruitcakes, personalised stationery (that will get used up), an item of fishing tackle that wears out. Or it might be a gift item, e.g. a cuddly toy, ornament, book, picture, which the customer decides to give to more than one person. Whichever it is, if you can come up with a repeat purchase item it can reap good profits in the future.

8. It should be an item which could be extended to a range

This is an extension of the above, in that you should always aim to sell something else to established customers. Your great advantage here is that they have already demonstrated their interest in your products and will be more likely to look at whatever else you offer. One way of doing this is to offer items that follow on logically from the first, e.g. you may have sold an enamelled brooch and you then offer earrings in the same design. You may have sold a book about golf and you then follow it up with a golf ball egg cup. The important point is that you have now identified your customers, and they now trust you, your products and service. The hardest part of the sale has already been overcome! Steer away from items that do not have an obvious 'extension' factor. There isn't much point in being a one-hit wonder.

9. A product which is legal

Make no mistake, if your product is not legal you will quickly be stopped by the authorities. Don't be tempted to cheat – it simply won't work. There are various rules and regulations covering mail order products. These include:

- the Sale of Goods Act 1979;
- the Trade Descriptions Act 1968;
- the Supply of Goods and Services Act 1982;
- the Mail Order Transactions (Information) Order 1976.

Copies of the above can be obtained from HMSO on 071-873 0011. You don't necessarily have to go through the whole of these documents. But if you are in any doubt as to your product's legality, consult the Office of Fair Trading (Tel: 071-242 2858). Not only do they produce a series of very clear leaflets on fair trading and consumer protection, they can also point you in the direction of further advice on a particular product.

Finally, most mail order sales/advertisements are further monitored by the Advertising Standards Authority and Mail Order Protection Scheme – see Chapter 6.

10. It should be something that will sell steadily throughout the year

Many mail order items are of a seasonal nature, e.g. Christmas gifts or gardening equipment. Wherever possible, try to find products which should sell all year. Toys, art and craft materials, clothes, books and hobby items are just a few suggestions. Otherwise, be prepared for seasonal highs and lows in your trading pattern. This may suit you. If so, all well and good – it certainly leaves room for other commitments. But if you want all year round trading, look for other related products that will complement your range, e.g. gardening gift items for September to Christmas; seeds from January to April; garden ornaments/furniture from May to September. Try and make your range logical and connected in some way. It will then appear more credible.

CHOOSING YOUR PRODUCT

A surprising number of items are sold through mail order and people do have success with some very strange products! But if you are starting out and looking for something to sell, there are certain categories of goods which are almost always popular with the mail order consumer and which display many of the characteristics discussed above. They are as follows.

1. Clothes

Clothes are the most popular mail order item of all and one which can sell well all year round. Women's and children's clothes are especially popular, and women are almost four times more likely to buy than are men! Clothes are also easy to package and send by mail. The only downside for a beginner is that you would normally have to take more (and therefore more expensive) advertising space to illustrate the item.

2. Gifts

This category covers a multitude of items and is particularly well suited to those manufacturing their own product – profit margins can be high and of course your item will be an exclusive. Personalised gifts are still quite popular – monogrammed slippers, engraved pens, initialled linen and the like. John Beale of Past Times has found this to be an important part of selling, giving the product a feeling of uniqueness and novelty.

Take note that sales of gifts can be seasonal, leaving you quiet in the summer and very busy in the run up to Christmas.

3. Gardening

The English person's fascination with gardening ensures that this subject will never die! But you do have to know your subject. Amateur gardeners would be unwise to try and sell plants through the post. They are a labour-intensive item and to sell them through mail order requires special skills. Yet profit margins on seeds can be very high, and there is an enormous and ever expanding choice of garden paraphernalia ranging from sun loungers to sundials, seemingly in constant demand. There is a woman in Devon who operates under the trading name of Lady Muck and sells manure by mail order! Apparently she is doing very well! A useful source of information for gardening ideas is *Making Money From Your Garden* (details on page 236).

4. Pets

Pets are another favourite topic with the great British public. Be careful that your chosen item is not readily available in pet shops, otherwise the customer will simply take note of your product and buy it locally. Books on animals and pets usually sell well.

5. Cosmetics

There are strict laws governing what you can and can't say about cosmetics and their properties. You would have to check very carefully with the ASA before running an advertisement for such a product. However, the quest for beauty is a constant one and these can be good products to sell. But you must have something different to offer, otherwise your customers will simply buy it in the shops. Yves Rocher is a good example of a cosmetics company selling successfully by mail order.

6. Health and fitness

Again, this category is strictly controlled by the ASA and other bodies, but it is a huge market. Items that sell well are vitamin pills, exercise equipment, skin treatments, and of course more personal items such as hair restorer, contraceptives and marital aids. Women in particular strive to conform to the accepted definition of beauty. Consequently, newspapers, magazines, television and radio carry countless ads promoting dietary aids; moreover, women make up the majority of the mail order market – 70 per cent of mail order items are aimed at women.

7. Hobbies and collectors' pieces

These make a good choice for mail order, provided you have sufficient knowledge of the item. Hobbies and crafts sell well because they are often specialist goods which are otherwise hard to obtain and can therefore be sold at a premium. You can also target your advertising to specialist publications, which may well improve your success rate. Popular hobbies and specialist areas include coins, stamps, bird watching, trains, veteran cars, vintage aeroplanes, genealogy, war memorabilia, dolls' houses

etc. Do be wary of selling anything with a very limited supply –
otherwise you will run out of product if not customers!

8. Foods

A very popular item, but not recommended unless you are
already in the food business, and able to handle the hygiene and
packaging requirements of perishables. Stilton cheese, smoked
salmon and hampers appear regularly as mail order offers,
especially around Christmas.

There are a few lines which the beginner could sell successfully; preserves, jams and fruitcakes in tins. The Collin Street
Bakery in Texas, USA mails out well over one million fruitcakes a year, most of them in the run up to Christmas, and sends
out to over 194 foreign countries.

9. Stationery

Stationery includes notepaper, cards, business letterheads and
pens. There is always a demand for upmarket paper and paper-
related items, especially when personalised. These are often
prestige goods and popular either as a gift or for personal use.
Paper items are also easy to pack and send. Some, for example
greetings cards, have a very high mark-up and can be sold all
year round (birthdays, Easter, Christmas, Valentine's etc.).
Charity catalogues often concentrate on these items.

10. Sports equipment

Always popular, not only for regular sports, e.g. football, golf,
fishing etc., but also for the many sporting crazes like
skateboarding and mono-skiing. Sports gear and related items
sell well at most times, both to the enthusiasts themselves and to
those looking for a gift.

11. Gadgets

A vast area that covers everything from executive toys to joke items, things bought essentially for their novelty value. However, we also live in a society which places great importance upon convenience, for example, automatic can openers, cordless car vacuum cleaners, automatic juice extractors and food processors all sell well. This would be a good choice for anyone with a new, exclusive or just plain clever product that can be sent through the post. If you are stuck for inspiration, look at the catalogues which come with the Saturday and Sunday papers – they are full of imaginative ideas.

12. Household

Another huge market that covers home improvements, interior decorating, furniture and furnishings – most household items are offered through mail order. Generally speaking though, they would need to have a degree of exclusivity or price advantage to make them successful as postal items. Also bear in mind the special packaging requirements of large items.

13. Books and information

This category is very suitable for several reasons (but then I would say that!).

- Books exist on practically any subject. You therefore have the scope to appeal to the widest possible audience.
- The content of a book can be very effectively described in a simple ad, without the need for an illustration.
- Most people buy a book at some time or other, either as a gift item or for themselves. Book buyers can also be good repeat buyers. Once again, the most successful titles usually appeal to the human desires mentioned earlier: health and beauty; general self-improvement; business and money-making opportunities.

- Most important, you have a choice of either 'buying in' books to sell on or publishing your own information; the advantage of the latter is that the perceived value of a book is contained in the information it holds; the book itself can be cheap to produce because it is the information people want and not a glossy production. Your profit margin can therefore be very high. You could sell, for argument's sake, a book at £12.95 which might have cost only £2 to produce – far outstripping the 3:1 sales/cost price ratios mentioned above.

If you have information which you think others might pay for, and feel confident about putting it down on paper (your printer can guide you with typesetting and design), then this is an excellent area to consider. But be absolutely sure that your subject matter passes the product analysis test. A book on the merits of the Underground system is not going to appeal as widely as a book on how to make money! Do think about whether or not people really want this information. No one could say that our *Government Auction Handbook* was a colour extravaganza or a masterpiece of literature. That wasn't the point. The information contained within that book was of great value and made it a bestseller. The number of copies returned to us by those who decided not to purchase that particular title were very low, which also goes to prove the point.

SOURCES OF IDEAS

You may have got as far as deciding which product area you would like to work in, but still be stuck for a particular item within that field. There are several ways to source ideas. Spend some time looking through the back numbers of newspapers and magazines. You could also try to get hold of any published reports on the mail order industry.

General newspapers and magazines

These are one of the best sources of mail order ideas. You should do the following.

- Look through back copies (the library often stocks these) and see what sold well several years ago. Sometimes these items can be resurrected, brought up to date and readvertised, e.g. a modern equivalent of the bullworker; the latest garden fertiliser etc. Most successful mail order items are cyclical and their themes eternal – health, wealth, power, prestige etc.

- Get into the habit of reading current magazines and newspapers to see what other people are offering. If you see something advertised regularly which also appeals to you, keep the ad and send off for it. When it arrives, assess its suitability as a mail order item. Did it travel well? Does it offer value for money? Could you expect at least a 3:1 ratio on the sales/cost price and could you source something similar or make it yourself? If the answer to these questions is yes, you may have found a good mail order product.

Specialist magazines, often aimed at the homeworker

There are several of these, for example, *Home Business* and *Home Run*, which are sources of ideas for products that can be sold from home. Subscription details at the back of this book.

Industry reports

On a more general level you could do well to invest in one of the industry reports published from time to time. For example, Mintel have recently produced one called 'Home Shopping Specialists', which looks at all aspects of the mail order industry, including which product categories sell best, who buys mail order most frequently and further defines the mail order consumer by age, sex, socio-economic group, marital status etc.

SOURCING YOUR PRODUCT

Hopefully by now you are closer to knowing what you want to sell, but may not have a clear idea of exactly where to find it. There are several ways of sourcing your product, some easier than others.

Manufacturers in the UK

The advantage of obtaining products in the UK is that you should have reasonable control over your supply. The best ways of locating a manufacturer are as follows.

- **By looking through trade magazines** for names and addresses of relevant manufacturers.
- **By scanning business opportunities** sections of national newspapers.
- **By looking up the companies and their products in trade directories.** For example, the *Kompass UK Register* is an enormous, 2-volume beast that lists details on over 40,000 suppliers of different products and services. It has a very comprehensive system of cross-referencing, so that you can source by product, company name, location, alternative suppliers etc. You should find a copy at most reference libraries. It is updated annually. Alternatively, *Kompass* costs £255. Publisher's details at the back of this book.
- **By attending trade fairs.** These are going on all the time – the National Exhibition Centre in Birmingham alone holds 100 major trade fairs every year. They are normally organised by theme, i.e. beauty products, crafts,

publishing, toys and are a terrific way for you to examine what the industry has to offer – under one roof on one day! The Exhibition Industry Federation publishes a free booklet called *Trade Fairs in Britain*, available from the EIF, details at the back of this book. It lists practically every UK trade fair for the year under product category and venue – an excellent source of reference.

Manufacturers abroad

Buying from manufacturers abroad is rather more tricky. The main advantage to you is that you could become the sole importer of the item and thus obtain exclusivity in the UK. You can also choose products from almost anywhere in the world. But the procedure is not without its risks. Your best bet is to work via the embassies; contact the commercial section and request the trade directory for that country. This should be sent to you free of charge. In it you will find a list of all the products of that country which are available for sale, together with the names, addresses, telephone and fax numbers of the companies concerned. You then contact the company direct, ask to be sent samples and a price list, and negotiate your terms direct with them. It then remains to organise shipment and you would be well advised to have the goods insured all the way to your door.

This may all sound relatively straightforward. But consider the potential pitfalls:

- you will be at the mercy of currency exchange rates, which can go against as well as for you;
- if your paperwork is not absolutely correct Customs and Excise can hold the goods until they are satisfied that everything is in order;
- you will have to plan at least three months in advance of your advertising campaign, to ensure that the goods are in stock on time;
- your shipment can be affected by adverse weather conditions;

- the manufacturers may change their line unexpectedly and you then have to start the whole selection process over again, but from a distance;
- you will probably be asked to pay for everything in advance, unless your bank has agreed to send confirmation that you will pay within, say, 60 days of receiving the goods.

It can be done, but think if there isn't a simpler way – at least to begin with.

Specialist mail order product wholesalers

The advantage of using these suppliers is that:

- they only sell goods for mail order;
- they act as wholesalers to people like you;
- they do not sell by mail order themselves and are therefore not in competition;
- they offer all the advantages of regular importers, whilst also negotiating exclusives on certain product lines;
- minimum quantities usually start small, so you can test a product before running a full campaign.

Two such companies are Sherelle International Ltd and Reuben Ash Ltd – addresses at the back of this book.

Publishers

Mail order books are well worth considering. If you want to sell someone else's books, the best way to source them is through a magazine like the *Bookseller*. This publication identifies publishers for you to buy from. It is published weekly by J Whitaker & Sons Ltd and is available on subscription. Tel: 071-836 8911 for details. Alternatively, browse in bookshops. Look for publishers who handle titles that interest you and track their telephone number through directory enquiries.

Once you have chosen a publisher, contact them and ask for their catalogue. Select your title, ring the publisher direct and tell them that you want to sell it by mail order. If they aren't already doing it, there shouldn't be any objection. Indeed, they should be delighted that you are offering to buy in bulk. Negotiate a price for a small test quantity (perhaps 100–200 copies). If these sell well, negotiate again on larger quantities. You will always be offered a minimum 35 per cent discount and maybe as much as 80 per cent depending upon the quantities you order, the publisher, the book and your powers of negotiation! Do ensure, however, that the book is up to date and that the publisher can provide you with ongoing supplies, preferably at short notice. You will also want to be offered any new titles, so that you can make further offers to existing customers.

Mail order is a good and somewhat underestimated method of selling books. Publishers are often forced to give their titles a rather short-lived sales campaign and then resign the books to their backlist. This doesn't necessarily mean that there is no life left in them and it is a great chance for you to capitalise upon somebody else's hard work! People who buy books by mail order are sometimes very different from those who buy from bookshops; so you could be opening up a whole new market.

Net Book Agreement

Do remember that you have to observe the Net Book Agreement when selling other publishers' books. This means that you have to sell at a cover price not below that set by the publisher. Not all books are subject to the NBA – check with the individual publisher. You will find that some books, especially those which have been in print a long time, have been taken out of the NBA and you can therefore set your own price.

Secondhand books

A special area of knowledge, but one well suited to mail order. If you are confident about handling second-hand books and feel that you know your market, a source publication is *Shepherd's Book Dealers in the British Isles*. It comes out annually and is available from any good bookshop or direct from the publishers (address at the back of this book). Currently priced at £24.

Making the product yourself

This usually applies to those working on a small scale, and offering craft and specialist items, e.g. toys, dried flower arrangements, handworked and leather products etc. Alternatively, you may have a large-scale manufacturing operation which you want to extend into mail order. Whichever, the advantages are the same:

- you can control and guarantee the supply more easily;
- the product is unique to you;
- the cost price can be closely monitored.

On the other hand, unless the product is already in existence, you will have to spend time and money developing the item. A sudden influx of orders may be difficult for a small operation to fulfil and others may copy your idea! Patenting is expensive and takes time. So, if you really want to sell your own product by mail order, be prepared to advertise aggressively and make as much money as you can as fast as you can. Alternatively, you have to dominate the market to such an extent that nobody else can muscle in.

4

YOUR PROFIT! SELLING AT THE RIGHT PRICE

IT IS VERY IMPORTANT to devote enough time to this aspect of your business. Pricing is the one area where you can't freely experiment – the advertising authorities frown upon it and the customer doesn't appreciate it. How would you feel if you bought a jumper for £20 and then saw it the next day for £15? So you have got to get it right first time. Selling at the 'right' price takes into consideration several factors and means selling at the price which makes you the maximum possible profit. To do that you have to understand the overall costs of your business.

THE TOTAL COSTS OF YOUR BUSINESS – DIRECT AND INDIRECT

The first point to understand is that your income from advertising is going to be your main or only source of revenue. This sales revenue has to exceed the total of all the costs involved in running your mail order business if you are to make an overall profit. These costs are both direct and indirect. Direct costs are those which relate directly to the manufacture and sales of your product. Indirect costs or overheads are those incurred in the overall administration of your business. In your mail order business the breakdown is likely to be as follows:

Direct costs

- the product (either purchase price or your manufacturing costs)
- artwork for advertisements
- advertising space
- delivery (if the item is purchased from a supplier)
- postage, packaging and fulfilment (when sending out to the customer)
- storage
- allowance for damaged or returned goods (generally allow 5 per cent of the sales price of the item, but this figure will vary depending on the category of product – clothes are often 10 per cent or more).

Indirect costs/overheads

- rent and rates (if applicable)
- stationery and office supplies
- insurance
- subscriptions to MOPS (Mail Order Protection Scheme) and other trade associations
- salaries (and PAYE and NIC where applicable)
- telephone/fax/photocopier
- gas/electricity
- legal fees
- accountant
- use of your car (if applicable).

It adds up, doesn't it? You have to be scrupulously honest with yourself about the costs of your business.

Moreover, if you already have a business don't be tempted to burden it with costs which really apply to the mail order side of the operation. Strictly speaking, you should apportion part of your rent, rates, salary, insurance, office administration etc. to your mail order accounts. Only then are you giving a true picture of its performance. After all, no one works for free in an office that costs nothing, so why pretend that this is the case with mail order?

WHAT YOU NEED TO CHARGE VERSUS WHAT THE MARKET WILL BEAR

So, with all these costs to consider it is vital to price your product correctly. To do this you have to balance two factors.

1. The price you need to charge

Most mail order products work on a 3:1 or preferably 5:1 ratio, i.e. the selling price is between three and five times the actual product cost. So, if your product was costing you £3, you would have to charge the customer somewhere between £9 and £15 for it. This is a fairly safe ratio for items in the £5–£50 range (which most of those new to mail order will be dealing with). With careful advertising it should mean that you can cover all costs and make a profit at the end of the year. Of course, the higher the ratio you can achieve, the more profit you can make. And the lower your product price, the greater volume you will need to sell to make decent money. Put another way, if you were selling jumbo jets by mail order, you could happily live off the proceeds of just one sale!

As an example, books are an excellent mail order product in that they quite often achieve a ratio of 5:1 or more; and if you decide to write and sell your own publications, you can achieve ratios of up to 10:1. Seed is another good product. Vegetable and flower seeds are often sold at up to 15× their actual cost! The trick is obviously to find products with a low unit cost; the Tin Pot Company very cleverly did this by taking plain tin watering cans and hand painting them to an exquisite finish. The cost of the can was relatively low, but the value-added factor of a hand painted finish was high.

2. What the market will bear

In tandem with the above you have to consider outside influences. What you need to charge has to be married with what people are prepared to pay. This is a combination of several factors.

What other people are charging for a similar product

You will probably have competitors selling a similar item and your price will therefore have to be within range of theirs. If it is much higher, the customer will obviously just go for the cheaper offer. However, this doesn't mean that you simply follow what everyone else is doing. For all you know your competitor may be paying much more or less for their product and advertising. You have to take into consideration your own costs as well. One thing is for sure, if your competitor is paying too much, they will soon be out of business!

An exclusive and unique product

You may have a product which is completely unique or with one particularly novel characteristic. Either way, no one else has it and you can therefore charge a premium. This might be because you are only offering a limited edition, of prints for example. Or because the item is unusual, like a giant vegetable seed range. Obviously, the price still has to be within reason. But you can still build in a little extra for that originality factor.

The psychology of your customers

Customers are fascinating creatures! They will pay for some things and not for others. They will pay extra for the convenience of mail order. They will pay if you have created such a desire with your advertising copy that they cannot resist the purchase. They will even subconsciously pay for the excitement factor of receiving a package in the post. But equally they have very definite psychological price barriers which you have no choice but to acknowledge:

1. **The £X.95 factor.** It only means five pence less to you, but to your customers there is a world of difference between £9.95 and £10.
2. **The different levels of resistance.** There are certain price brackets that people seem consistently to reject. Anything up to £15 is fine, but £15–£19 is more tricky (£19.95 seems to be acceptable); £20–£25 is OK, but £25–£29 can be awkward (£29.95 is fine). It obviously varies depending upon the product, but look closely at ads and you will see far more products at £12.95 or £14.95 than you will at £16.95 or £18.95. In addition, even numbers are usually preferred to odd, i.e. either £12.95 or £14.95 is more attractive to the customer than £13.95. For most mail order purchases the upper level of resistance is £50 – few people will spend more than that on a mail order item, except where payment is in instalments. And from your point of view, it is very hard to make money selling items at less than £5, simply because of the volume of product you would have to sell.
3. **The 'five pound note' factor.** People also seem to find it easier to accept a price if they can envisage it as a note. Anything priced around £5, £10 or £20, particularly £5 and £10, seems somehow inexpensive because it is just the equivalent of a small piece of paper. Strange but true. I often go to car boot sales and watch people making their purchases. They are almost cavalier about anything costing £1. 'After all, what is a small coin?' they seem to

be saying. But charge them 90p or £1.10 and they
hesitate.
4. **Odd and even numbers.** Sometimes an 'offbeat' amount
can be more convincing to the customer. If you charge,
e.g., £14.76 for an item, it can appear more genuine than
if you just plump for £14.50. The customer assumes that
you must have had specific reason to charge that amount
and that the price is therefore fair. Not everyone favours
this approach, but some do and have success with it.

A WORD ABOUT PRICE TESTING . . .

Price testing is not strictly illegal, but neither is it encouraged.
The only hard and fast rule is that if you offer the same item in
different areas of the press at the same time, but at different
prices, the public are entitled to request that you refund the
difference if they have bought the item at the higher price.

. . . AND PRICE INCREASES

Everyone has to increase their prices at some time or other. If
you had a shop you would simply change the price tickets. In
mail order there is a three-month rule which states that any
advertiser is bound to honour the price set in their advertisement for up to three months after it has appeared in the
press. If someone orders the goods after that time, you can write
and inform them (if applicable) that the price has changed. This
comes under the terms of the Advertising Standards Authority
(more in Chapter 6).

So, all these factors have to be considered when pricing your product, so that you are selling at the right price. There is no magic formula to tell you how to ensure an overall profit at the end of the year. That of course depends on:

- your level of success with each individual advertisement (Chapter 11);
- your control of overheads (Chapter 5).

5

SETTING

UP

S O, YOU'VE TACKLED one of the fundamental parts of mail order – selecting and acquiring your product. Now you have to organise your working environment and, most important, your bookkeeping. Please don't ignore this chapter if you are already in business. There are several sections where the advice is specific to mail order, not least the information on accounts.

YOUR TRADING STATUS

However simple the business, there are certain formalities which have to be observed when setting up. One of them is your trading status. If you are already in business this will not be an issue; you simply continue with the system you already have in place. If you are just starting out, however, there are several options, each with different legal and tax implications. Here are the ones that are most relevant to mail order.

Sole proprietorship

A sole proprietor or sole trader is an individual who works for him or herself (but may also have employees). It is the simplest business to set up and you can start trading without any special legal formalities. All the profits are yours and you pay income tax on them as a self-employed individual. You are also liable for any debts in the business and can have personal assets seized to meet them. You can trade under your own name or one which describes your business, e.g. The Garden Gnome People. It is not obligatory to register a trading name, but you should check with Companies House in Cardiff to make sure that your chosen name is not already in use.

Most people setting up a mail order business will choose to be a sole trader. It is simple to set up and if you decide that mail order is not for you, it is equally simple to dismantle.

Partnership

A partnership is formed when two or more people agree to share the profits, losses and risks of a business (in any proportion they agree upon). A partnership is recognised in law even without any written agreement between the partners, but it is obviously advisable to have an agreement drawn up by a solicitor. Each partner is *personally* responsible for *all* the debts incurred by the business and can have their own assets seized if the other partner has insufficient funds. Income tax is paid on the individual's share of the partnership profits. Lastly, a partnership can trade under a different name from that of the partners themselves.

You may choose this form of trading if you want the support of another person or some financial input. Whichever, you are strongly advised to agree your terms on paper, even if your partner is your husband or wife.

Limited company

A limited company is a separate legal entity in its own right. Its owners (of which there have to be at least two) have paid money into the company in return for shares and are called members or shareholders. On a day-to-day basis the company is run by a board of directors – in a small concern they are often the members/shareholders as well. A limited company pays corporation tax on its profits. These profits belong to the shareholders, who will then pay personal tax on them as well if they are distributed as dividends.

There are both advantages and disadvantages to setting up a limited company.

Advantages

1. Shareholders are not personally responsible for debts run up by the business. They can only lose the money that they have put into the company.
2. Suppliers sometimes prefer to do business with a limited company because they see it as something more tangible and secure. It is therefore often easier to get credit and set up trading accounts.
3. Customers reading your mail order advertisements may feel happier about sending money to a limited company (not that it actually offers any greater protection, but it improves their perception none the less).

Disadvantages

1. A limited company costs money to set up and run. It can either be set up by your accountant or you can buy 'ready-made' companies from company transfer agents. This can cost as little as £80 (see the Business Opportunities sections of the national newspapers). Limited companies are governed by strict rules in the Companies Acts, and involve quite a lot of administration. Among other things, you have to file annual independently audited accounts with the Registrar of Companies. These are open to public inspection. You have to hold regular shareholder meetings and keep detailed minutes of these.
2. Company directors have to assume special legal duties and responsibilities. Should a director be found negligent on

these, they can be held personally responsible for company debts. Quite often these days, directors are also required to give personal guarantees for loans made to the company.

If you are new to business and to mail order, it is probably better to start out as a sole trader or partnership. It is the simplest way to operate, and involves less cost and time spent on administration. (You can always become a limited company when the business is established.) The only drawback is that you will probably also get less favourable credit terms from suppliers – at least until you have established a track record. Give this careful consideration, because it affects the financial input required from you.

Whichever form of trading you choose, begin by setting up a bank account. This will either be in your name, your trading name or as a limited company. You will need a cheque book, paying-in book and *weekly* bank statements. If you already have a personal bank account, you might find it helpful to set up the business account with the same branch; it will probably make the bank feel more comfortable about your operation. In return, ask about free banking for small businesses. Many banks now offer this for the first year of trading.

If you are expanding an established business, you can incorporate your mail order finances into existing accounts. However, you should set up separate columns in your books, so that you can properly monitor the independent performance of the mail order operation; otherwise you are in danger of obscuring the true results of your new venture.

YOUR 'OFFICE'

The flexibility of mail order is no more evident than in your choice of office premises. If you already run a business and just want to add the option of mail order sales, simply set aside space within your existing premises, preferably a separate room. If, however, you want to start from scratch while maintaining your current job, set aside a room (or rooms) at home and call it your office. Of course, you could go the whole hog and rent office space; there are some great deals to be had, especially if the business doesn't rely upon a prime location, which mail order does not. But you would be wise to wait for that until you are more established. Office rent is just another fixed overhead you don't need and working from home is very convenient. In the meantime, start being nice to your postman, who will be delivering the lifeblood of your business!

You should also invest in one or two good small business handbooks, which will give you further details on setting up successfully (details at the back of this book).

It is important that you tell everyone else in the house that the room you have set aside is your office. Make sure that they understand and accept the implications of your working from home and the potential disruption they may face. You will be receiving and processing money, handling customer information and maybe even sending out the product from that room. Ideally, it should be kept locked when not in use. And you must make a mental division. Remember, when you are in there, you are doing business!

The equipment you will need

There really isn't very much required and you probably have most of it already.

Telephone

If working from home you could use your existing telephone and apportion part of your bill when keeping the books. If this isn't practical, have an extension fitted. In an office environment you simply use or add to the existing telephone system. Whichever you have, make sure that anyone ringing in receives a professional response. Answer the phone using your mail order trading name. If you are at home, don't allow children to take calls. An answering machine would be useful when you are not available. Having said that, it is unlikely that many people will call you (unless you include a telephone number in your advertisement – more about this in Chapter 7). But *you* will need to use the phone, mostly to book advertising space and to order up any supplies you need.

Files

It is essential that you keep all documents organised and safe. Your paperwork will consist mostly of the following.

1. Customer and general correspondence I keep all customer correspondence alphabetically by surname and for at least two years. You will find that people write in on all manner of topics – queries, seeking advice, sometimes just wanting a chat! Pay attention to these letters, since they offer a fascinating source of information and ideas.

2. Advertising material Advertising material should be kept indefinitely. You will want to refer back to it when writing new copy and may need to correspond with the advertising authorities at some point. This is a very important file. You should also get into the habit of cutting out and keeping ads that you see in the papers; either for products similar to your own or just ads that you think are effective and eye-catching. They will be a helpful source of reference.

3. Customer coupons/letters Customer orders and the coupons/letters that they send in should be stored with great care. Keep them filed by product and within that, in sealed plastic bags – one for each advertisment you run. Mark the date and name of the newspaper on each bag. As your business expands you may have to find separate storage space for these coupons.

4. Suppliers' invoices Invoices for goods you have bought should be kept alphabetically by supplier's name; we shall handle these in more detail later in this chapter. Needless to say, all files should be kept safe. Your bookkeeping, cheques, paying-in books and bank statements should be kept locked away if possible.

Stationery

If you are already in business and if it is practical, use your current trading name and address for your mail order operation; you can then continue to use your current stationery. For those starting out, don't splash out on expensive stationery until your business is well established.

Start off with the basics: some headed paper for general correspondence and some compliments slips for shorter notes will be enough. Plain black print on white paper is quite acceptable. Include your business logo if you have one. If you are a sole trader, you will need to print your trading name and address, and if you wish, your telephone number. Be aware that if you are printing your home address, you may get a few callers/ enquirers at the door, usually people who live locally and recognise the address. If you are a limited company, your company name, address, country of registration, registered address and number of incorporation (this last piece of information is given to you when you first register as a limited company) must be included. Any printer can advise you on the design and layout of your stationery. Some high street instant print shops specialise in this area.

It is not a good idea to use a PO box number on your stationery. People don't generally like or trust them and it could affect your sales. It is much better to stick with your home or company address.

Access to a fax and photocopier

It isn't essential that you have these in your office, but access to them would be helpful. I use the fax when confirming advertisement bookings. It is faster than confirming by post and vital when I am taking last-minute space, as some newspapers insist upon a fax confirmation before running an ad.

Computer

See Chapter 9 for more on the need for a computer. In the
meantime, if you do not already have one, don't worry; a good
typewriter is fine for everyday correspondence. If you *do* have a
computer, you will want to use its word-processing facility –
mainly for keeping customer names and addresses.

If you are operating from just one room, divide it into three
areas: have one section for your desk, telephone, files and
paperwork; another for storage of your product; and a third for
packaging and fulfilment. Space will be at a premium, so keep
everything neat and tidy. If at all possible, use two rooms, one
for storage/fulfilment and the other for administration.

Think big!

You may be starting out on a small scale, you may be operating
from just one room, but that doesn't mean that you have to
appear small-time as well. The beauty of mail order is such that
you can be a one-man band, and still project the slick and
polished image of a much larger company. It is your efficiency,
service and professionalism that will be assessed by the outside
world, not the size of your shop front or premises. Nobody can
see you. They don't know that you are operating from a room
6 ft square! So decide from the outset that your standard of
service will speak on your behalf; in the eyes of the outside
world you will be up there with the big operators.

Credit cards

You should consider offering your customers the option of
paying by credit card. Not only will it maximise your potential
business, but will also make you appear a larger and more established operation. You may already have a business which offers
the use of credit cards. If so, just extend the practice to your
mail order operation. If not, look into it. Some businesses find
that credit card sales make up over half their volume, particularly with more expensive items.

The procedure varies slightly from bank to bank but is basically as follows. Almost all banks have an internal credit card division, which holds a licence both to issue credit cards and process credit card transactions. You cannot approach a 'credit card company' as such, but go to your own bank and tell them that you want to offer credit card facilities. Access and Visa are the most common cards used, and should be sufficient to start with. The bank will then appoint a credit card representative to come round and discuss the details of your business and assess your suitability. Most banks will want to see a 12-month trading history or at least some sort of financial records before approving your application. This may make things awkward for those starting out, but a good personal banking history may help your case – and applications are meant to be considered on individual merit. You will be asked for details of your background, financial resources etc.

If your application is accepted it will take six to eight weeks to process. You will then receive a pack which will include everything you need to process credit card orders. It only remains for you to include the appropriate details in your advertisements – something we shall look at in more detail in Chapter 7.

Don't be put off by the administration involved. Credit cards are pretty simple to handle and well worth it in terms of the extra business. Remember though, there is always a price to pay. In the case of credit cards you will probably be charged a fee of between 3 and 5 per cent of your credit card turnover. This also has to be built into your calculations.

YOUR LEGAL RESPONSIBILITIES

If and when you take on employees to help with your business, you will need to comply with the Health and Safety at Work Act 1974. Your place of work must be healthy, safe, have proper lighting, ventilation and heating – ask your local health and safety inspector for advice.

You will also need employers' liability insurance. If you are working alone this will not apply, but do insure the office and its contents, particularly if you are holding stock there. Your insurance premiums will vary, depending upon whether your office is situated within your home or elsewhere. Do watch out for the specially tailored policies that now exist for home businesses (see back of book for details).

Should you decide to rent office space, contact your local economic development officer for advice on premises and financial assistance. If you are in a rural area, the Rural Development Council can sometimes provide purpose-built units and help with loans, grants and advice. Anyone with fewer than 500 employees is also entitled to seek assistance from the Department of Trade and Industry Enterprise Initiative.

YOUR ACCOUNTS

You are now ready and raring to go. But don't try to sell anything until you have set up a proper bookkeeping system. Accurate bookkeeping and accounts are vital to the success of your mail order enterprise. If you have previous business experience, this section will help you by highlighting aspects specific to mail order. If you have none, make sure that you fully understand the advice given before proceeding to Chapter 6.

Very few people enjoy doing their accounts. It always seems to be an area that worries them, especially when running their own business. Of course you should be concerned; correct accounting will highlight potential problems early on and help you to make the right financial decisions. But it shouldn't fill you with dread. It really isn't difficult to keep your books properly and mail order is such a beautifully simple business that your books can be simple too. Look on it as the key to your success rather than a chore and make sure that you are completely organised before running your first advertisement.

Call in the experts

Accounting is one of the few areas of your business where you should consider using the services of an expert. How much you use them will depend upon whether you have chosen to be a sole trader, partnership or a limited company.

As a sole trader, you need an accountant to check your books and prepare accounts at the end of the financial year and maybe help prepare your personal tax return. If you are completely new to business, I would suggest that in addition to your daily bookkeeping you do monthly accounts as well; this would comprise a profit and loss statement, and a balance sheet. It is imperative that you are able to keep track of the overall performance of your business. In Chapter 11 we will see how to assess the individual performance of each advertisement. But in any business there will be many overheads, and you will only make an overall trading profit if your advertisement profits cover all these expenses and leave some money over. Your business will be on a small scale to start with and not involve many transactions. Some people consider it unnecessary to go to the trouble of monthly accounts. However, I think you should do them, even if they are very simple. Get your accountant to check over them as well, at least for a few months: first to make sure that you are preparing them correctly and second to highlight any potential problems you may have overlooked.

As a limited company you will need your annual accounts audited. The audit has to be prepared by a registered, qualified accountant and will obviously cost more than your accounts as a sole trader.

Do it yourself . . .

There is really no need for you to employ someone to keep your books on a day-to-day basis. Quite apart from the expense, it is important that you learn to understand the figures. In any case, no one will ever care about your business quite as much as you do. What you must pay out for, however, is a few pounds' worth of advice before you start up. Agree with your accountant how best to keep the books so that he will be happy with them at the end of the year. In the long run, this saves money. Expert help and advice on tax and VAT are also essential. There are various allowances and schemes available which can reduce your tax liability and help with VAT cash flow.

If I were starting out in business today, I would prepare all my questions and then buy one or two hours of my accountant's time. If you don't already know of a good person, ask among your friends for recommendations or make enquiries at the local chamber of commerce. At the back of this book you will also find the addresses and phone numbers of various institutes of chartered accountants.

TAX

Before looking at your bookkeeping and accounts, it is important to understand your obligations to the Inland Revenue. Your tax liability will vary depending upon the trading status you have chosen. But whichever that is, you must register it with your local inspector of taxes. Equally, both you and anybody else in your employment will be liable to National Insurance contributions, which are handled by the DSS (Department of Social Security). So you will have to inform your local DSS office as well.

Tax for sole traders and partnerships

As a sole trader or partner you are liable for tax on the profits of the business. Your own allocated salary will be taxed as part of these figures and you will also have to pay National Insurance contributions.

The actual amount of income tax you have to pay in any year will depend upon the amount of your profits and on any other taxable income you may have – but rates start at 20 per cent and increase to 25 and 40 per cent. Your tax is due for payment in half-yearly instalments on 1st January and 1st July, starting from the year in which operations commence.

It is worth remembering too that there are certain expenses which can be deducted from your business income before calculating your taxable profits (ask your accountant about these). If your allowable deductions exceed income, you will have made a loss and this can be set off against any other income you may have, to reduce the tax on it.

Tax for limited companies

A limited company pays corporation tax on its profits. As a director you are still technically regarded as an employee; your salary and bonus are allowable deductions in computing those profits but you will pay income tax on them as an employed individual. Both employer's and employee's National Insurance contributions will have to be paid on your salary as a director. Corporation tax is at rates commencing at 25 per cent and increasing to 33 per cent, depending upon the level of profit of the company. It has to be paid no later than nine months after the date of the accounts.

PAYE

If you are a sole proprietor and no one else works for you, you do not need to run a PAYE scheme. Otherwise, all salaries, including those of directors, and wages, including monies paid to casual workers, are subject to PAYE. You can either run the scheme yourself or get your accountant to handle PAYE. Either way, you should get the *Employers' Guide to PAYE* information pack from the Inland Revenue to enable you to register. Employers' National Insurance contributions are also deducted and collected through the PAYE system. Note that if you are a limited company, the tax office dealing with the company's tax affairs might be different from the one that deals with your PAYE.

VAT

VAT need not be a particularly complicated area, but the penalties for handling it incorrectly are stringent, so the services of an accountant to help get you started are highly recommended.

When should I charge VAT?

If your turnover exceeds, or is estimated to exceed, the annual limit set by the VAT office every year, you have to register for VAT and charge VAT on your sales. The VAT rate in 1993 is 17.5 per cent of the price of the product. The limit for 17th March 1993 is £37,600 and applies regardless of your trading status. If your turnover is below the limit, you can choose whether or not to register for VAT. If you are selling to the general public, it would not normally make sense to register as you would have to increase the amount customers pay by the amount of VAT. There are, however, some items which carry a VAT rate of zero (as I write, this includes books) and in these cases it may make sense to register for VAT even if your turnover is below the statutory limit. Again, your accountant's advice will help you to decide whether the financial benefits justify the additional administration required.

You must be sure that your product is correctly classified before you start trading. Your local VAT office will tell you whether or not it is VATable. It must be stressed that ignorance is not accepted as an excuse. If you sell a VATable item without charging the customer VAT, you will be asked to give back the equivalent of the VAT element, regardless of the fact that you have never had the money.

How to register

Your first job therefore is to register with your local VAT office. You will be issued with a VAT number, which must be shown on all sales invoices and credit notes (obviously in the mail order business you won't have many of the former). Once you are registered, you will have to complete a VAT return, usually each quarter.

It is certainly possible to complete your own VAT return. Many people do and the VAT office supplies comprehensive notes to help you. But it is a good idea to ask your accountant to show you how to do the first one or two returns.

ORGANISING YOUR BOOKS

Accurate books are the key to managing your business (quite apart from being a legal requirement). Knowing how to analyse each advertisement and determine whether or not it is making money is obviously very important in helping you to decide where to advertise next (see Chapter 11). But at any given time you should also be aware of the following.

- **The big picture,** i.e. whether or not you are still making money after all the other expenses/costs involved in running your business are deducted from your revenue.
- **How much cash you have in the bank,** to enable you to plan day-to-day expenditure, so that your cheques don't bounce!
- **What you owe your suppliers,** to keep a check on expenses and stock levels.

- **What is owed to you**, normally a low figure in mail order because the customers have sent their money before the product is dispatched.
- **Your other liabilities**. This is an important one, particularly in mail order. Remember that you are receiving money **in advance**; so at any given point you will most likely have to allow for the cost of product and fulfilment needed to honour orders already paid for but not yet dispatched.

The books you need to keep

If you are already established in business or a limited company and have a system, that's fine. You need simply to add an extra set of analysis columns to your daily cash book and remember to flag any item which relates to the mail order side of your operation. It is unnecessarily complicated to run a completely separate set of books and bank account. But you must be able to separate out the figures to gauge the progress of the mail order division. You should in any case look at the systems suggested below, as they will help focus your understanding of mail order bookkeeping.

For those who are new to accounts here are six systems that are particularly useful:

- cash book;
- weekly housekeeping account;
- order book;
- purchase and sales invoice file;
- monthly profit and loss account;
- monthly balance sheet.

You can keep your books manually or on computer. Unless you are computer literate and confident about operating a package, it might be easier to keep manual accounts. Whichever you choose, you should agree with your accountant the exact structure of the books/accounts before you start trading.

Cash book

The cash book records for every trading day the money coming into and going out from the business. Your receipts on any day would include all the cheques and cash you deposited at the bank that day, and your payments would include all cheques you issued and cash payments you made.

Accuracy of the cash book is essential as it forms the base from which several of the other systems are derived and it should be reconciled with each bank statement, which I suggest be requested weekly. Differences between your cash position as shown in the cash book and on your bank statement should be explained by items (cheques and cash) that have yet to be presented to or cleared by the bank, and items such as bank charges and standing orders that are charged directly to your bank account.

Weekly housekeeping account

Cash is the major concern of almost all businesses and, while the cash book provides the exact situation at a particular moment, once a week I take this a step further by subtracting from the cash book balance the value of all items (including VAT payments to be made to the Customs & Excise) that I shall have to pay but have yet to be invoiced.

This is very much a worst scenario as it ignores the fact that some of your purchases will be held as stock and have a resale value. It provides, however, the full extent of your liabilities and often identifies problems in time for you to deal with them, while taking less than half an hour to complete.

Order book

This is simply a record of everything you have ordered. It helps focus your mind on exactly what you are spending money on and is very useful when compiling the housekeeping account.

Your order book is best kept on A4 paper in a lever arch file, alphabetically by suppliers' names, allowing one whole sheet for each supplier and recording:

- the date that you placed the order – useful to know if there is a dispute or query;
- exactly what you ordered;
- how much of the item you agreed to buy;
- the price you agreed to pay;
- whether or not the invoice has been received.

Purchase and sales invoice files

These are files of the actual invoices you have received or have issued. Again, I would use a lever arch file and divide it into four sections, one each for paid and unpaid purchase invoices, paid and unpaid sales invoices. I always file alphabetically by name of supplier and chronologically within that. Whenever an invoice is paid, mark the date and cheque number on the invoice so that you can trace the payment, if necessary.

Monthly profit and loss account

Your daily cash book and weekly housekeeping account will certainly help you keep costs under control and avoid nasty surprises. But you also need a regular summary of what you have made or lost each month. A monthly profit and loss account will help you monitor your progress until the end of year accounts are prepared.

Your profit and loss should be made up to the last day of each month. Basically, you want to compare your income (sales) against your expenditure (cost of sales and overheads). What is left should be a positive figure and is your monthly profit! All the totals needed can be obtained from your cash book.

There is more than one way to construct a profit and loss statement, and you should discuss with your accountant the layout most appropriate for your business. The layout I use comprises three main categories.

1. **Net Sales** The total proceeds received from the sale of products less the total of any refunds issued plus any other sources of income such as name rentals (see Chapter 12).

2. **Cost of sales**   Those costs directly incurred in generating
   the sales and normally including product or raw material
   purchases, advertising and dispatch costs (or the
   fulfilment house's charges). Remember to adjust for the
   stock at the beginning and end of the period.
3. **Overheads**   Those costs incurred as part of being in
   business and little affected by the level of sales achieved in
   the month. They would normally include salaries, rent
   and rates, telephone, electricity, stationery, insurance and
   fees.

If you have registered for VAT you should exclude the VAT
element from all of your figures, but if you have not, include the
figures without any adjustment.

The difference between net sales and cost of sales is often
referred to as gross profit. This should be examined carefully
and compared to the previous month's figures. If your gross
profit as a percentage of sales has dropped significantly, you
should ask why. Have you spent more on advertising but not
had a comparable increase in sales? Have your fulfilment costs
gone up? Whichever is the case, it is an important danger signal
and you should attempt to remedy it immediately.

Gross profit less overheads is usually referred to as operating
profit, i.e. what is left at the end of the month after all expenses
have been deducted (except for any interest on money
borrowed). Again, it is useful to compare this with the previous
month's performance.

Some of your overheads, like electricity, telephone and bank
charges are normally paid quarterly. You must therefore realise
that some months will show an unusually high overhead figure
and allow for the fact that the bill refers to a period of three
months but has been posted into one.

As a mail order business (and very possibly working from
home), your overheads should be low. Your major expenditure
will come in 'cost of sales' and it is your gross profit figure that
requires close attention. Keep an eye on the refunds as well –
are they increasing out of line with sales? Lastly, watch these

sales figures. You will need to know what is the correct sales/advertising cost ratio (see Chapter 11), and you should be aware of this figure when examining sales revenue.

The balance sheet

The balance sheet is a 'snapshot' of what your business owns (assets) and what it owes (liabilities) at a fixed point in time. It not only tells you whether or not your business is solvent, but also gives important information on the nature of your assets and liabilities. Balance sheets normally take into account the following.

1. **Fixed assets** Assets that have a long life (normally years), such as your items of equipment and furniture. In your case, the value will not be significant, especially if you operate without a computer.
2. **Current assets** Items with a short life (normally months), stocks, debtors (including VAT) and any cash held at the bank. In an emergency, the quick realisation of these current assets might generate less cash than shown on the balance sheet. Could you sell the stock easily and at what price? Could you collect from your debtors? (There shouldn't be many in a mail order business). Is your money in the bank accessible? (Remember BCCI!)
3. **Current liabilities** The amounts you owe your creditors, including the Inland Revenue and any overdraft you may have. Unfortunately, in an emergency, you will have to pay all of these.
4. **Net current assets** This is the difference between the total current assets and the total current liabilities. It is the amount of money you have available now with which to run the business.
5. **Total assets less current liabilities** These are the fixed plus current assets minus the current liabilities, i.e. the net worth of the business.
6. **Financed by** This is a term which appears at the bottom

of the balance sheet and tells you where the 'net worth' comes from. Some of it will be profits, a cumulative figure brought forward from month to month. If you are a limited company, some of it will also come from share capital put into the company.

Your business is technically solvent if its assets are greater than its liabilities; in other words, if it has a positive net worth.

WHY YOU NEED NEVER GO BUST

Many businesses fail because their cash flow is bad. That is to say, they are unable to pay their bills because monies owed to them have not been paid on time. The sad fact is that you can be making a profit and still fail because of bad cash flow. With mail order you shouldn't have this problem, because the customer has to send in money before you dispatch the order. It is a very simple system which immediately eliminates the problem of cash flow.

Forward trading

But, and there is always a but, this so-called advantage shows up one or two difficulties as well. Always be aware that cash coming in to your business will have to be followed by product/fulfilment costs going out of the business. It is easy to get carried away with the excitement of cheques dropping out of envelopes and forget that you then have to fulfil the order – and that costs money. This becomes especially important when you do your profit and loss accounts. If, for example, you had an ad which came out at the very end of the month, you might only have received orders/money by the time the profit and loss is put together, and not allowed for the fact that you might have to buy in stock to fulfil the orders – a cost that should be taken into account and which could seriously affect your profit and loss figure. So do allow for this in all your calculations. Don't be caught out!

Allow for refunds

Lastly, you should always make a 5 per cent allowance for refunds. That is to say, allow for the fact that up to 5 per cent of your customers will want their money back. For some mail order products, e.g. clothes, the figure can be much higher (10 per cent or more). This is money which will have to leave the business subsequent to its having come in as an order. Make provision for it.

The detail in this chapter is included so that you can ensure your enterprise is based on solid financial systems. Absorb this information carefully before moving on. It is vital if you are to control your mail order millions!

6

COPING WITH REGULATORY BODIES

SO FAR, we have looked at all the reasons why mail order is such a good business to go into and why it is relatively easy to do so. This is all great stuff, but consider for a moment the possible negative implications. If almost anyone can start a mail order business, it follows that one or two might be less than honest. You have chosen to play by the rules and may therefore think that this doesn't affect you, but it does. If the actions of a few give the mail order industry a bad name, your sales will also suffer. Remember that your customer cannot see you to know that you are one of the good guys. If they have been cheated by someone else, they may just assume that you will do the same and decide not to order. It would be a great shame if this alone caused you to lose sales, especially since you have worked so hard to get everything else right.

Luckily for us all, this is where the industry's regulatory bodies step in.

WHO THEY ARE

The mail order watchdogs (not their official title!) are a group of independent bodies, each of whom is involved in regulating different aspects of the direct mail industry. The following are the ones you are most likely to have contact with:

- the Advertising Standards Authority (ASA);
- the Mail Order Protection Scheme (MOPS);
- the Data Protection Registrar (DPR).

WHY THEY EXIST

The short answer is 'not just to make life awkward for you!' Far from it. Each of these bodies performs various functions which include:

- giving official recognition to particular aspects of mail order;
- providing a forum for discussion of industry issues;
- protecting the rights of the consumer;
- advising and informing the trader/advertiser;
- curbing bad practice among traders/advertisers.

In essence, they act as a sort of referee between government and trader, trader and customer, ensuring that all legislation and business is conducted fairly and in the best interests of all parties concerned. It is quite a tough act, but one which is vital if the mail order industry is to maintain a positive image and encourage people to use its services.

WHAT THEY DO

Each body performs very different tasks, so it is best to take them one at a time.

ASA

Advertising Standards Authority

The ASA acts independently of both the government and the advertising industry. Its major task is to protect the public by ensuring that all advertisements appearing in the UK (except those on television and radio) are 'legal, decent, honest and truthful'.

To this end, anyone who prepares or publishes advertisements (and that includes you of course) has to follow the rules laid down in the British Code of Advertising Practice. There is no formal 'membership' as such – no one pays a fee to join. The 'Code' works on the basis of self-regulation, that is to say, the advertisers take it upon themselves to uphold standards in advertising. You agree to assume personal responsibility for demonstrating the truth of your claims and to 'observe the Code's rules in the spirit as well as the letter' (taken from *Advertising Under Control, a guide to the ASA*). The idea is both to show goodwill to the public/consumer and to avoid legislative intervention by the government wherever possible. The Code is actually published by CAP, the Committee of Advertising Practice, a body responsible for 'reviewing, amending and enforcing' the Code, and which is itself supervised by the ASA.

The Code of Advertising Practice
The Code is a long and detailed document. It is none the less essential that you understand and follow its principles when

writing advertisements. Failure to do so can land you in a lot of trouble. At some stage in your career you should read it in full, but to get you started, I have extracted the sections most relevant to you as a mail order operator (taken from a summary of the British Code of Advertising Practice, printed as part of *Advertising Under Control, a guide to the ASA*):

All advertising should be:

- legal, decent, honest and truthful;
- prepared with a sense of responsibility both to the consumer and to society;
- in line with the principles of fair competition generally accepted in business.

Introduction

The Code is the body of rules by which the British advertising business has agreed that the overwhelming majority of the advertisements it produces should be regulated.

The Code establishes a standard against which any advertisement may be assessed. It is a guide both to those concerned with commissioning, creating and publishing advertisements, and to those who believe they may have reason to question what an advertisement says or shows.

The Code is applied in the spirit as well as the letter.

Scope

- Advertisements in newspapers, magazines and other printed publications.
- Advertising material such as brochures and leaflets or newspaper/magazine inserts.
- Advertisements in media principally intended for circulation outside the UK.
- Packages, wrappers, labels, tickets and the like, except to the extent that they are depicted in an advertisement, in which case any words, pictures etc., which are reproduced in a legible or otherwise comprehensible manner are subject to the Code.

Definition

For the purposes of the Code:
- A *product* is anything that is capable of forming the subject matter of an advertisement. It is most often a tangible object of trade, but may also be, for example, a service or facility, an idea, a cause or an opportunity.
- A *consumer* means any person likely to be reached by a given advertisement (and not only a member of the general public, or one of those directly addressed).
- A *claim* is to be understood as applying to both *express* and *implied* claims.

Interpretation

The opinion of the ASA on any matter concerning the interpretation of the Code is final.

Conformity with the Code is assessed in the light of an advertisement's probable effect when taken as a whole, and in context. In applying these criteria, particular attention is paid to:

- the characteristics of the likely audience for the advertisement;
- the medium by means of which the advertisement is communicated;
- the nature of the advertised product;
- the nature and content of any associated material made available contemporaneously to consumers by the advertiser.

General rules

Primary responsibility for observance of this Code falls upon advertisers, and remains with them even when delegated, for practical purposes, to an advertising agency or other intermediary.

Substantiation

Before offering an advertisement for publication, the advertiser should have in his hands all documentary and other evidence necessary to demonstrate the advertisement's conformity to the Code. This material, together, as necessary, with a statement outlining its relevance, should be made available without delay if requested by the ASA.

Legality

Advertisements should contain nothing which is in breach of the law, nor omit anything which the law requires.

Advertisements should contain nothing which is likely to bring the law into disrepute.

Decency

No advertisement should contain any matter that is likely to cause grave or widespread offence. Whether offence is likely to be caused and, if so, of what gravity, will be assessed in each case in the light of the standards of decency and propriety that are generally accepted at present in the United Kingdom.

Honesty

No advertiser should seek to take improper advantage of any characteristic or circumstance which may make consumers vulnerable; as, for example, by exploiting their credulity or their lack of experience or knowledge in any manner detrimental to their interests.

The design and presentation of advertisements should be such as to allow each part of the advertiser's case to be easily grasped and clearly understood.

Truthful presentation

No advertisement, whether by inaccuracy, ambiguity, exaggeration, omission or otherwise, should mislead consumers about any matter likely to influence their attitude to the advertised product.

Testimonials

Except when the opinion quoted is available in a published source, in which case a full reference should be made available on request, the advertiser should be able to provide substantiation for a testimonial in the form of a signed and dated statement, containing any words which appear in the advertisement in the form of a direct quotation, and with an address at which the author of the statement may be contacted.

Recognisability

An advertisement should always be so designed and presented that anyone who looks at it can see, without having to study it closely, that it is an advertisement.

Guarantees

Words such as 'guarantee' should not be used in an advertisement if, in consequence, there is any likelihood of consumers mistakenly believing, when such is not the case, that it is the advertiser's intention to confer on them, or procure for them, a legal right to recompense or reimbursement.

Where it is intended that such a legal right be created, it should be made clear to consumers, before they are committed to purchase, whether their right lies against the advertiser or against a third party (as it may do, for example, where insurance schemes are used to prolong warranties).

Availability

Advertisers should be able to show that they have reasonable grounds for supposing that they can supply any demand likely to be created by their advertisement.

Products which cannot be supplied should not be advertised as a way of assessing potential demand.

Fear and distress

Without good reason, no advertisement should play on fear or excite distress.

Violence and anti-social behaviour

Advertisements for weapons and for items such as knives, which offer the possibility of violent misuse, should avoid anything, in copy or in illustration, that may encourage such misuse.

Protection of privacy and exploitation of the individual

. . . advertisements should not portray or refer to any living persons, in whatever form or by whatever means, unless their express prior permission has been obtained.

Denigration

Advertisers should not seek to discredit the products of their competitors by any unfair means.

Imitation

No advertisement should so closely resemble another advertisement as to be likely to mislead or confuse.

Direct response advertising, marketing and mail order

All mail order and direct response advertisements should indicate the period within which the advertiser undertakes to fulfil orders, or, when appropriate, provide services. Except in certain circumstances, the period should not be greater than 28 days from receipt of order.

All reasonable steps should be taken to ensure that lists and databases used to market consumer products and service are accurate and up to date, that they avoid duplication of mailings to the same name and address and that prompt action is taken, upon request, to correct personal information.

This is only a summary of the Code, but it should give you a feel for what the ASA are trying to achieve. Do make sure that you read all their material, preferably before you start trading.

Follow the code when writing ads

Advertisements are examined in more detail in Chapter 7. But if you ever have any doubts as to the content of your intended advertisement, you can ask the ASA for its advice – that is another of their primary functions. This advice is free. If you publish an advertisement that contravenes any part of the Code, intentionally or unintentionally, you are more than likely to be challenged. Any member of the public can write to the ASA with a complaint about an ad. The ASA considers over 150,000 advertisements each year as part of its monitoring programme. So, don't think that you will escape unnoticed!

What happens if your advert is the subject of a complaint?

You do, of course, have rights of your own. It is not unknown for people to manufacture a complaint about an ad in the hope of disrupting a competitor's campaign! But in all cases, whether fair or not, there is a set procedure which has to be followed.

The ASA will write to you and question the particular claim. The onus is then upon you to prove to the ASA that your claims are true. You will be given a number of days in which to reply and, normally, your advertising can continue while this correspondence goes on. Often, the ASA will accept your explanation and decide not to act. But in 25 per cent of cases, they uphold the complaint. You will then be asked to change or remove the ad immediately. If you do not, the ASA can publish details of their judgment in their monthly report, circulated throughout the industry. Word gets round and you may find that newspapers etc. become reluctant to sell you further space. Persistent failure to comply with the ASA's requests could even land you in court. So do pay great attention to your advertisements.

The Mail Order Protection Scheme

MOPS was set up in 1975 to protect customers who buy mail order products as a result of advertisements in national newspapers. The scheme aims to reimburse readers under certain conditions:

- if the advertiser goes bankrupt, into liquidation or ceases to trade and therefore cannot supply goods already paid for by the consumer;
- if the advertiser fails in business and therefore cannot provide a refund for goods already returned.

MOPS only deals with national newspapers, not local papers, magazines or periodicals; MOPS only refunds customers who have bought from advertisements in publications which are members of the scheme. It also covers all display ads which ask for all or part of the customer's money before the goods are dispatched. Its current newspaper membership is as follows:

*Evening Standard, Financial Times, The Times, The
Sunday Times, Guardian, Independent, Daily Telegraph,
Sunday Telegraph, Observer, Daily Express, Sunday
Express, Star, Independent on Sunday, Daily Mail, Mail
on Sunday, News of the World, People, Daily Mirror,
Sunday Mirror, Daily Record, Sunday Mail, Today, Sun.*

This list includes the papers themselves and their associated
magazines.

Membership of MOPS is compulsory for anyone advertising
in national newspapers (either direct or through a media buyer/
agency – see Chapter 8) and requesting cash with the customer's order. To join you have to complete a set of application
forms (available from MOPS) which will then be vetted by the
Secretariat of MOPS to ensure that you are fit to conduct a mail
order business. This takes about 28 days. The forms will ask
you about your financial status, past business record, product,
premises, advertising copy, stock levels etc., and must be
answered fully. Don't worry if you are new to business. This
shouldn't jeopardise your application. If you use a media
buyer/agency you will also have to complete a form on their
behalf, without which the national newspapers will not accept
bookings for ad space.

If for some reason your application is rejected, you do have
the right of appeal. Upon joining, your membership will be
renewed annually and your fee calculated according to your
projected annual advertising expenditure. This falls into the
following bands:

Fee	Advertising expenditure
£175	£10,000
£350	£30,000
£650	£60,000
£1150	£100,000
£2000	£300,000
£3000	£500,000
£5000	£500,000 plus

(1994/5 figures)

Anyone starting up will fall into the £175 bracket, but be aware that the advertising expenditure quoted refers to 'published rate card' (PCR), that is, the full rates asked by the advertising media. After your first year in business, MOPS will calculate your membership on the full rate card value of space taken in the previous year. They do not take into account the fact that you will have negotiated large discounts on the PRC (more on this subject in Chapter 8).

When you become a member you undertake certain obligations; the most important ones for you to remember are as follows:

Obligations of members

6.1 Members undertake to adhere to MOPS terms of business as notified to them in writing by the Managing Committee and to support this guide in the spirit as well as in the letter.

6.2 Members must advertise with the public interest in mind and all advertisements will be legal, decent, honest and truthful.

6.3 Members are required to comply with the British Code of Advertising Practice and the British Code of Sales Promotion Practice administered by the Advertising Standards Authority.

6.4 All advertisement copy must contain in legible size the approved MOPS logo or the initial MOPS.

6.5 The logo must only be used by an approved advertiser in a 'cash off the page' advertisement in a member publication.

6.6 The logo must not be used adjacent to, or be construed to form part of any guarantee given in the advertisement.

6.7 The logo must not be used in any classified advertisement which is not display or semi-display [i.e. an advert which is just lineage], or in any literature or headed notepaper of the advertiser.

MOPS also publishes a list of general rules which you will find cropping up again and again in mail order practice. For that reason, I am listing them here in full (taken from the MOPS guide):

General rules

7.1 A member shall not submit for publication a misleading advertisement nor give false or misleading indications as to price, worth, value or quantity.

7.2 Every advertisement will, in the body copy, contain (amongst other things) the corporate identity of the advertiser and the full postal address at which he may be contacted. Accommodation addresses must not be used.

7.3 In the case of a sole proprietor the full name of the individual and the full postal address must appear in the body copy, in the case of partnerships the names of the partners (up to a total of nine) should appear to identify the 'Trading Style'.

7.4 These requirements do not preclude a member from also stating in an advertisement another address to which orders may be sent, i.e. Freepost etc.

7.5 If a coupon is used in an advertisement this should be viewed as an order form under the Companies Act and the registered number of the limited company, if applicable, should appear therein.

7.6 Each advertisement must contain details which make clear in what period of time the order will be fulfilled, i.e. allow 28 days for delivery.

7.7 The fulfilment period for any order should not without MOPS written approval be longer than 28 days except in the following circumstances:

    a) Bespoke goods.

    b) When a series of items are to be dispatched in sequence only the first item must be dispatched within 28 days. The intervals between dispatch of the following items must be shown clearly in the advertisement.

    c) Plants, shrubs, etc.

7.8 Should it become clear that the order cannot be fulfilled within the stated period the advertiser must immediately offer the respondent a refund, should they none the less elect to wait they should either be given a firm date for the alternative dispatch of goods, or the progress of their order should be notified at regular intervals.

7.9 Upon the receipt of a request for a refund this should be made as soon as reasonably practicable and should include any expenses incurred in the return of the product.

7.10 Credit notes must not be issued in lieu of refunds under any circumstances.

7.11 Nothing in any advertisement or catalogue should lead readers to believe that their rights at law are in any way diminished or removed.

7.12 The full name and/or trading style of the advertiser must be displayed by way of a permanent visible sign at the trading address of the advertiser.

7.13 A responsible person must be available at the full postal address given in the advertisement and the goods advertised must be available for public inspection during normal business hours.

7.14 Advertisers must carry adequate insurance to cover fire (premises and stock), burglary and theft of stock in transit.

7.15 The advertiser must have possession and/or control of the goods to be sold and must hold sufficient quantities to meet the reasonably anticipated demand of the advertising campaign.

7.16 Forward trading, that is receiving customers' money then purchasing goods to fulfil orders, is not allowed. Discovery of such conduct will lead to the permanent suspension of the advertiser.

7.17 Switch selling, that is substituting one product for another will not be accepted.

Play by the rules

It is very important that you understand and follow the above
rules and regulations. MOPS is there to help and guide you, but
it also has the power to recommend to all member publications
that they refuse your advertising if you do the following.

(a) Breach the British Code of Advertising Practice, or the
British Code of Sales Promotion Practice.

(b) Breach the MOPS rules.

(c) Generate an unacceptable number of complaints.

(d) Fail to notify MOPS of any change in company structure or methods of business.

(e) Non-payment of additional Central Fund fees [payable
if your advertising exceeds the band chosen at the
beginning of the year].

(f) Non-submission of audited accounts when due or
requested.

(g) Misuse of the MOPS logo.

(The above is quoted directly from section 5.12 of the MOPS
guide.)

This could effectively put you out of business. So do take your
membership seriously. It all adds to the credibility and reputation of the mail order industry.

The Data Protection Registrar

This area only affects you if you intend to:

● hold customer data on your own computer;

● employ a bureau to hold your customer data on computer.

The Data Protection Act 1984 aims to protect the rights of those whose personal information is stored on computer and to regulate data users (those who record and use personal data). A data user can be a company, corporation or an individual. As a mail order operator you are most likely to become a data user; if you hold the personal data of your customers (i.e. names and addresses) on either your own or somebody else's computer, you must register with the Data Protection Registrar. Small businesses can join by completing forms DPR4 (available from the Registrar's office, address at the back of this book). The registrar will want to know:

- about you;
- the data you hold;
- what you use that data for;
- where you intend to get the information from;
- to whom you intend to disclose the information;
- any overseas countries to which you propose to transfer the data.

With mail order, it is most likely that you will get this information from customers responding to your ads and disclose the information to anyone subsequently renting your mailing lists (see Chapter 12).

The Registrar has the right to refuse your application if you give insufficient information. Once accepted, you have a legal obligation to comply with the eight Data Protection Principles designed to protect the rights of the individuals whose personal data you have recorded (details sent to you upon registration). Failure to do so could lead to your registration being cancelled in part or in whole: it would then be a criminal offence to continue holding personal data. Registration is very straightforward in practice and, of course, it is essential that you register.

OTHER ASSOCIATIONS

There are several other organisations with whom you may come into contact, but do not have to be a member of. The most likely are the Periodical Publishers Association and the Newspaper Society. The former represents magazines and the latter, regional and local newspapers. If you (or your media buyer) wish to book advertising in any of the above media you should contact the paper directly. But they may well ask you to provide an undertaking, fill out forms providing details of your financial position, your ability to fulfil customer orders and may take up references or make additional checks. This is standard procedure and, again, the forms are simple to complete.

HOW NOT TO FALL FOUL OF THE SYSTEM – ASA, MOPS AND THE DPR

The best way to keep within the system is to comply with the rules and regulations of each body. But you should aim to do slightly more than that and cultivate a good overall relationship with these associations. Never forget that the ASA, MOPS and the DPR are there to help and advise you, as well as to regulate your activities. In any case, you should be pleased that they do, because it all helps to give the industry a positive image and maintain consumer confidence, without which you don't have a business! Be co-operative and helpful, and you shouldn't have any problems.

One last word: all the information quoted in this chapter and sent out by the relevant associations is subject to amendment and change at any time. Make it your responsibility to keep up to date with new legislation. Ignorance is no defence.

7

ADVERTISING: YOUR SHOP WINDOW TO THE WORLD

THIS IS ONE of the most important chapters in the whole book. You shouldn't even think about running a mail order offer before understanding the principles laid out below. Your advertisement is your shop window to the world. It is 'salesmanship in print' – your principal vehicle for selling a mail order product. A good mail order advertisement will have your customer rushing to catch the next post. Allow them the slightest doubt and you have probably lost the sale. The truth of the matter is that you can sell a less-than-perfect product with a great ad. But you will rarely sell a great product with a bad ad and you certainly won't realise its potential. It could well mean the difference between your success and failure. That's my official wealth warning.

The good news is that you don't have to be called Saatchi to create a winning advertisement. Mail order is very much a science and the basic principles of good copywriting can be mastered by any determined person. I cannot guarantee you success every time, but the following rules and tips will dramatically increase the response to your ad, whatever the product.

HOW TO WRITE AN
ADVERTISEMENT THAT SELLS

Opera lovers will be familiar with *Aida*; so are copywriters, as it also stands for:

- **Attention**
- **Interest**
- **Desire**
- **Action.**

These are the four essential elements of any advertisement. They must all be present together in a successful piece of copy.

Attention

The sole purpose of a headline is to make the reader read further. You simply have to grab the customer's attention. Not only is the typeface therefore larger than that of the rest of the advert, but the message has to be clear. You have only a few seconds and even fewer words in which to:

- establish the reader's interest;
- convince them that there is 'something in it for them';
- persuade them to read further.

I cannot over-emphasise how vital your headline is. Seventy per cent of ads fail because of a poor headline. If it doesn't tempt the customer, your campaign ends right there. It is also important to realise that there will be other products similar to yours being sold by mail order (if there aren't – remember Chapter 3 – you may have something to worry about) and it has to be your product, not the next one, that gets sold. It doesn't matter what the product is, the principle is the same. Your headline has to stop the readers dead in their tracks.

There are certain standard words which often appear in headline writing. They are as follows:

Now . . .	**Power . . .**
Secrets . . .	**New . . .**
How to . . .	**Hurry . . .**
Make money . . .	**Easy . . .**
Save . . .	**Amazing . . .**
Learn . . .	**Quick . . .**
Don't . . .	**Why . . .**
Discount . . .	**Bargain . . .**
You too . . .	**Why not . . .**
The best/worst . . .	**Free . . .**
Success . . .	**Special offer . . .**
Do you want . . .	**Claim your . . .**

You can see how these words would appeal to the customers' emotions and encourage them to read on. Incorporate such sentiments into your headline whenever possible.

Look back to our giant tomato ad on p. 33. A boring headline might have read: **'Delicious tomatoes!'**

So what? The tomatoes I buy at the supermarket are delicious. Our headline read: **'This is the best darn tomato I've ever tasted!'**

It was catchy, funny and instantly challenging to any tomato grower. It played upon the gardener's desire for status and success. We sold seeds to over 50,000 customers in under four months. Even Bernard Levin, the columnist, was moved to write a piece in *The Times* about our tomatoes. Recognition indeed!

The curiosity factor

In essence, your headline must excite the curiosity of the reader. Another of our products, a book about the serious but relatively unknown subject of the prostate gland, was entitled: 'What every man over 40 should know . . . now'.

We had to be deliberately obscure because we knew that although the prostate gland is an important area of men's health, few would have understood the word 'prostate' as a headline and would therefore have read no further. It was our job to encourage the relevant people to read on, even if they didn't yet know that they were the relevant people! Again, the book sold and continues to sell thousands of copies with just that simple but intriguing headline. So don't limit your potential readership before you even start. Make the headline appeal to as many people as possible and go from there.

This last example illustrates another important point about your headline. Most classics of advertising mention the product in the headline, but you do not have to include a full description of the item. Indeed, sometimes it is better if it isn't mentioned in detail, as again, the reader just has to carry on in order to find out more. There was an advertisement in the paper recently entitled 'Summer or winter. No one takes off more'. It was actually giving information about holiday price reductions. Quite apart from the sexual innuendo it was simply intriguing and I'm sure made many more people read the ad than if they had just written 'Look at our holiday discounts'.

So your headline must:

1. be punchy, positive, grab the reader and encourage them to read on;
2. be quite short (two or three lines at the most, but one is better);
3. include some of the 'instinct' words mentioned above;
4. excite curiosity;
5. engage the reader's emotions;
6. it does not have to be complex, indeed, it shouldn't be;
7. it does not have to make reference to the product.

Here are some examples of effective headlines and a short explanation of the reasons for their success.

1. **'Read and make money'** A brilliant headline. Short and to the point. Everyone wants to make money, so the maximum audience will read the ad. Anyone who has got that far is obviously capable of reading and will therefore consider this an easy way to make some spare cash. It is instantly appealing and to a wide audience. It is actually advertising a proof-reading business.

2. **'How to talk to your cat'** This is one of our own books – about communicating with your cat! The headline makes the reader feel that the product will give them special information that will enhance their understanding of their pet. A catchy and quirky title, it aroused a lot of press interest and generated sales of over 50,000 copies of the book.

3. **'They laughed when I sat down at the piano. But when I started to play!'** This is a very famous headline, written by John Caple, which sold thousands of 'teach yourself' music courses in America. It is basically a great storyline and goes on in full-page detail to tell how the 'little' man teaches himself to play music and becomes the envy of his neighbourhood – a modern-day morality tale if you like.

4. **'Be a successful writer. Make money writing – even while you are learning'** This is another very good headline. Lots of people dream of becoming a writer, simply for the cachet. To make money as well, even while a beginner, is beyond most people's expectations and would definitely pull a response.

Finally, here are some headlines from the past which worked wonders for other advertisers. Notice how they all engage the reader's emotions – it would be difficult not to read the ad having seen the headline:

- **Do you make these mistakes in English?**
- **You can laugh at money worries – if you follow this simple plan.**

- **When doctors 'feel rotten' this is what they do.**
- **How I improved my memory in one evening.**
- **How I made a fortune with a 'fool idea'.**
- **'I lost my bulges . . . and saved money too!'**
- **Imagine me . . . holding an audience spellbound for 30 minutes!**
- **It's a shame for you not to make good money – when these men do it so easily.**
- **67 reasons why it would have paid you to answer our ad a few months ago.**
- **Are they being promoted right over your head?**

(Source: *How to Write a Good Advertisement*, by Victor O. Schwab)

So, now that you have your potential customer's attention you must use the next part of the advertisement to maintain their interest and create a desire for the product. Read on . . .

Interest

This forms the major part of the advertisement – otherwise known as the 'body copy'. So far you have managed to halt the reader's progress through their paper/magazine. Now you have to go into much more detail, and explain the various features and benefits of your product, presenting your information in such a way that will keep the reader interested and encourage them to proceed to the next phase – that of desire. There are six issues to remember when writing body copy.

1. Credibility

Your information must be credible. This is both a legal and a practical requirement. Over-exaggeration and ceaseless enthusiasm will lack conviction. The 'I am the greatest' style of advertising doesn't work because no one will believe you. Be honest and, wherever possible, stick to specific information rather than generalisations. 'Lots of people buy this product' is not as convincing as '2,500 people have bought this product in the last three months'. Specific figures sound much more credible. To cut a long story short, if your advertisement was believable your customer would be happy to pay £50 for the product, not the £10 you are asking for and not getting! Your reader has to believe that this product really is going to be as good as you have suggested. They have to trust your information, and will then be happy and keen to buy, at which point the price becomes less important. So stick to the facts. If you don't, you'll not only upset your customer, but the Advertising Standards Authority as well.

2. *Benefits to the customer*

Every product has a set of characteristics or benefits. These features are what makes a product individual and you should use the bulk of the advertisement to list them in some detail. By the time you have finished describing the various benefits the reader will be faced with a multitude of reasons as to why the product is relevant to them and not one suggestion to the contrary! In doing so, you are also answering many of your readers' possible objections to the product, leaving the way clear for them to buy. You must always remember to tell the reader what's in it for them. They are, after all, acting out of self-interest. If you don't, you will appear to be just selling to them and they will resent this straightaway. For instance, if you're advertising a vacuum cleaner with a revolutionary cleaning mechanism, don't just say that and no more. Go on to explain how this will make the machine more effective, less noisy, cheaper on electricity consumption, easier on the carpet etc. Stick to the truth but try to bombard the customer with the benefits as well.

3. *Your USP*

Most important of all, you must decide upon the USP, the unique selling point of your product, something no other rival has got. You may have gone most of the way to convincing your customer that the vacuum cleaner is terrific; but if you can add that it is the only vacuum cleaner in the UK which has, for example, two dust bags, you will have more chance of closing that sale. It is also worth mentioning that the USP can be factual, as above, or imaginative. This is where 'creative copy-writing licence' comes into play. In the famous series of ads for chocolates we were led to believe that a man had leapt off cliffs, out of aeroplanes, grappled with alligators and arrived unruffled to deliver chocolates (which were still intact in the box). Well hardly! But since it did not transgress any of the ASA laws, it was acceptable – and probably boosted the sales of the chocolates.

4. Style

Equally important is your style of writing. Ideally it should be chatty, almost colloquial. This doesn't mean that all adherence to spelling and grammar can go out of the window. Instead, you should try to imagine you are in conversation with a good friend; you no doubt speak easily and fluently with them, and your copy-writing should be no different. It should flow without awkward pauses, be personal, friendly and on the level of the reader, not condescending. It may not be perfectly grammatical, but it must have pace, pulling the reader along. Sentences should be short and to the point, as should paragraphs. There is no place for hyperbole in copy-writing and every word must be made to work. Space costs money and you want to get across the maximum message in the minimum number of column centimetres.

5. Bullet copy

When you are listing the benefits of your product you can either take one short paragraph per point or, for even greater impact, use 'bullet copy'. This is simply a list of black spots or asterisks set on the left-hand side of the page, followed by the benefits, for example:

- Look great!
- Feel wonderful!
- Increase your energy levels!
- Get rid of stress!
- Eat well!

You'll be more successful with your writing when you subscribe to our bi-monthly magazine *Freelance Writing & Photography.*

We'll show you:

- **how to write what editors want**

- **what the market is looking for currently**

- **where to send your work for the best chance of success**

- **markets you've probably never heard of**

- **tips which will improve the quality and saleability of your writing.**

To subscribe send a cheque for £16.50 - or for further details send SAE to:

Freelance Writing & Photography
(Dept. Begs.)
Tregeraint House,
Zennor, St Ives,
Cornwall,
TR26 3DB.

Tel. (0736) 797061.

An example of an advertisement using eye-catching bullet points.

The slogans on page 104 could, for instance, be advertising a health product.

Some adverts are composed almost entirely of bullet copy, with a short introductory paragraph and response mechanism to top and tail it. Bullet copy is most effective as it gives only the important information, cutting out all unnecessary extras, and you will find that it is sometimes just one specific point that appeals to the customer and persuades him or her to buy.

6. The direct approach

It is also usually better to address the reader direct, for immediacy, than to write in the third person. This engages the reader. You are talking to them, not their neighbour. You should also use the active rather than the passive form of the verb – for the same reason. 'It is said that Nuglo works wonders . . .' is not as effective as 'We say that Nuglo works wonders . . .', or even better, just 'Nuglo works wonders . . .'.

If you have brought the reader this far, your potential customer has more or less decided to purchase the product. Now you have just one more bridge to cross . . .

Desire

Reiterate the benefits

You are now about 70 per cent of the way towards making a sale. You have fully described the product and all its benefits. This in itself has started to create a desire in your potential customer. But you just have to help them along the final stage of the journey and reiterate the benefits of the product. The customer wants to be reassured that they are making the right decision in sending off their money. Don't let them down now.

You need only to add a short paragraph at the end of the body copy – simply pick out the major advantages of the product and list them again. For example: 'Remember, when you buy the Maxi Barbecue you are buying reliability, top quality design and good looks into the bargain'.

Remember, too, that people buy with their emotions. Look

how many travel agents sell Paris on the strength of its romance factor. We sold thousands of tomato seeds, partly by describing how luscious the tomatoes would be, not to mention the envy they would arouse in non-gardening neighbours. So, don't forget to establish desire for your product. It is the essential link between interest and action.

Action

Action stations! You have successfully lured the customer right through the advertisement. Don't blow it now by making it hard for them actually to buy your product. Your 'response mechanism' must have certain essential ingredients.

- **Your business name, address and postcode;** so that the customer knows where to send the order.
- **The name, address and postcode of your customer;** so that you know where to send the product. (It is amazing how many people send money and absolutely no form of identification.)
- **Simple instructions on how to pay;** you might want to extend this section if you are offering a special rate for multiple purchases.
- **A code for you to identify the source of an order;** this is most important. The code identifies which paper the response is derived from and so helps you work out which is the most successful advertising medium. To make life easy, use a code related to the name of the paper and date of the advert, for example: MOS/12/03 = *Mail on Sunday*, appeared 12 March. You can do this with any paper: *Independent* = Ind; *Telegraph* = Tel; *Sunday Express* = SE, etc.

Where you place your code will depend upon which type of advert you are using. If you opt for an editorial look response mechanism (see below), the code should appear as part of your address, ideally as a department number e.g. Dept Ind/12103. This means that the customer will automatically include it when sending off their order. It also means that when you receive your orders it will be immediately obvious from the envelope which particular advertisements they come from.

If, however, you are using a 'coupon' response mechanism (see below), the customer need do nothing, as your code will be printed within the coupon. All a customer does is cut out the whole coupon and send it off. The source of the order will not be obvious until you open the envelope and look at the coupon. To make this process easier, always put the code in the same position e.g. the bottom right hand corner of the coupon. You then know exactly where to look and will not waste time searching around.

- **Details of delivery time;** apart from being a legal requirement, it makes good marketing sense to reassure your customer that they won't have to wait long for their purchase. In fact, the faster you deliver, the higher the chance of selling something else to the same customer.

- **A money-back guarantee;** again, this makes the customer feel secure about sending money for something they have not seen to someone they do not know. It is normal to offer a 30-day money-back guarantee. In America this approach proved so successful that many companies offer indefinite guarantees. Their returns are so low that they can afford to do this.

- **An 'opt out' clause;** this is required by law, if you intend to rent out your customer names to other companies (see Chapter 12). You can either word this as suggested below or print a box for the customer to tick if they do not want to receive any more offers. You are then under a legal obligation to remove from your computer the name and address of anyone who requests it. Failure to do so is an infringement of the Data Protection Act.

Fitting the information in

It might seem that you have a lot of information for you to squeeze in, but in practice it is really quite simple. You can use one of two approaches.

The first method is to adopt the 'editorial look'. This is better used when you want to keep the advert looking informal and 'newsy', and when your customer is only paying by cheque or postal order:

> Simply send your name, address and cheque for £12.95 (incl of p&p) to Smithco Ltd, Dept Ind/12/03, 37 Jones St, London SW2 1AP, allowing up to 21 days for delivery. You may return the product for a full refund within 30 days if not completely satisfied. We hope to be able to make a variety of further interesting offers from reputable companies. If you prefer not to receive such offers please write to Smithco Ltd at the above address.

The second method is to use a response coupon.   These are generally found in larger ads and take up more room. Ads using response coupons are therefore more expensive, but are necessary if you want to offer the customer the option to pay by credit card; this expense can pay off. Many people like to pay by credit card because of the safety and convenience factors.

A coupon is also more likely to ensure that the customer will give you all the correct information you need. A typical coupon might look like the one shown overleaf.

If your customer is responding to an editorial advert you will obviously receive a letter addressed to Smithco Ltd, Dept/12/03 etc, with a note inside requesting the product, together with a cheque/PO. Don't bin the envelope until you have made a note of your identifying code, otherwise you won't know where the order came from! (It may sound obvious, but it is infuriating when you forget to do it.) A good idea is to transfer the code on to the customer's note; then you have all the customer information together and ready for later analysis.

If, on the other hand, the customer is responding via a coupon, they will simply cut it out and pop it in the envelope (always make things easy for the customer). If they have completed all the sections correctly, all you have to do is keep the coupon safe. Even your code will be there, usually in the bottom right-hand corner.

To: Smithco Ltd, 37 Jones St, London SW2 1AP
Please rush me ____ (product name and quantity) at £__
(price) each (incl p&p) on the understanding that if not
delighted I can return it within 30 days for a full refund.

☐ I enclose my cheque for £___
(payable to Smithco Ltd)
or
☐ Please charge my credit card/account no:

THE NATIONAL NEWSPAPER
MOPS
MAIL ORDER PROTECTION SCHEME

☐☐☐☐☐☐☐☐☐☐☐☐☐☐☐☐ Expiry date . . ./. . .
(Visa/Access)

Name _____**BLOCK**

Address _____**CAPITALS**

_____

_____Postcode _____**PLEASE**

Signed _____Date _____MOS/22/01

Regd No. 1111111

Please allow up to 30 days for delivery. We hope to be
able to make a variety of further interesting offers from
reputable companies. If you prefer not to receive such
offers, please write to Smithco Ltd at the above address.

One word of warning – do make it easy for the customer to
write clearly by giving them enough space on the coupon and do
stipulate the need for block capitals. Otherwise you or your fulfilment house will be wasting time and money trying to deci-
pher names, and the customer may not receive their order if the
package is incorrectly addressed.

SOME RULES OF WRITING ADVERTISEMENTS

There are a few general points which must be observed when
writing advertisements.

1. You must display your MOPS logo when advertising
   'cash with order' products in any national daily, national
   Sunday or colour supplement paper which is a member of
   the MOPS scheme. This is for your protection and that of
   the customer. If you fail to do so, the MOPS committee
   can recommend to the newspapers that they shouldn't
   accept your advertising. Remember that this ruling does
   not apply to the local press and the smaller magazines.
   Always check to make sure you know which media
   currently come under MOPS.
2. If you are a limited company you must display your
   company registration number within the coupon. You can
   make this pretty small and unobtrusive; one way is to
   print it along the vertical side of the ad.
3. You must also show your trading name and address both
   inside and outside the coupon, so that if a customer needs
   to contact you after sending off the order, he still has a
   copy of your address with the rest of the ad. If you are a
   limited company, the address outside the coupon must be
   your registered address.
4. It is always a good idea to copyright your work. This is
   very simple and can be laid out as follows:

   © Smithco Ltd, 1993, 37 Jones St, London SW2 1AP
   © Name of co/year/registered address of company

   This is a straightforward formula, which is usually
   centred just above the coupon and below the body copy,
   in small print. It becomes especially important when you
   find a winning product. We were able to stop more than a
   dozen 'copycats' of our advertisement for the bestselling
   Government Auction Handbook – these people would
   otherwise have simply copied our ad and defrauded us of
   business.
5. Postage and packing; p&p must be clearly stated in the
   advertisement in the same size and colour print as the
   price itself. If the price quoted is inclusive of p&p, this
   must be equally clear.

6. VAT cannot be shown as an extra to the stated price, but neither do you have to say that VAT is included in the price.
7. Some advertisements carry telephone numbers for people to place orders direct. This is not advisable unless you have the human resources to spare. It is now law that any advertisement telephone number has to be manned during office hours. Not only is this costly, but it is not always the case that telephone numbers actually bring in more business; it might come in more quickly, but not necessarily in greater volume overall.
8. One of the ASA rules is that an advertisement should look like an advertisement, i.e. it shouldn't mislead the reader into believing it to be a news story. If your advertisement strays into this category you should put the word 'Advertisement' above the headline. It can be in small print, but it has to be there.

YOUR ADVERTISEMENT CHECKLIST

Here is a checklist of things to remember when writing an advertisement.

- **Headline, body copy, response mechanism**   the three essential sections of your ad.
- **Attention, interest, desire, action**   the four essential responses you must elicit from your reader.
- **Benefits**   never forget that the customer wants to know what's in it for them. When you have written the ad, read it through as if you were the customer. If you aren't persuaded to buy the product yourself, then the ad needs rewriting.
- **Honesty**   you are, of course, allowed to sing the praises of your product, but do keep it within the realms of

reality. The Advertising Standards Authority can ask you to provide backup evidence for any of the claims made in the ad, and if you cannot provide it, the ad can be banned.

- **Style**   Remember to KISS (Keep It Simple Stupid!). Use short, easy sentence constructions; keep the pace going; give specific examples wherever possible (to heighten the reader's interest). Give customer quotes wherever possible. Make every word work for its living and be really mean about space. If you are worried about writing in this style, start by just putting down everything you want to say, and then go back over it, ruthlessly pruning those unnecessary words.

- **Ease of response**   hold your customer's hand right to the end. Make the response mechanism clear and easy to follow. If you make it hard for people to send you money, they might just not bother.

ADS THAT WORKED . . . AND WHY

To illustrate good copy in practice, two of Carnell's most successful adverts are reproduced on pages 114 and 116, and analysed below.

Bullet copy – Health Tips

A   The headline is going to appeal to a wide range of people because it is very general and about something which people deem important, i.e. their own well being.

B   The first paragraph uses emotive words – New, Vital and Latest – to grab the customer's attention. It also holds on to the maximum readership by confirming that it is a book for everyone interested in health. Who isn't?

C   The bullet points allow us to put across lots of benefits without taking up too much space. They are wide-

A # HEALTH TIPS

B A NEW BOOK REVEALS VITAL Health Tips based on the latest nutritional and scientific findings and time-proven remedies. This book is of vital importance to everyone interested in their health. Here are a few tips covered in this *Complete Handbook Of Health Tips:*

C
- How to get more energy and combat fatigue (2 nutrients may help).
- How to flatten your tummy with a 20 second, daily exercise.
- A nutrient that may help improve memory.
- How to deal with stress, including what nutrients may be helpful.
- A nutrient that may increase resistance to disease.
- 4 simple ways to take off weight.
- The only effective way to get rid of cellulite.
- 4 tips for relieving canker sores.
- A cheese that can help prevent tooth decay.
- A herbal remedy to prevent migraine headaches.
- One doctor's way to prevent grey hair.
- How to get rid of face hair.
- How to shorten miseries of a cold.
- 3 tips for relieving sinus congestion.
- 5 ways to stop foot odour.
- 3 nutrients to minimise harmful effects of alcohol.
- 2 vitamins that may help avoid bruises.
- 5 ways to relieve haemorrhoids.
- How to relieve nightly leg cramps.

- Prostate trouble: A simple tactic to alleviate getting up nights.
- A nutrient that may help lower blood pressure.
- 4 tips to fall asleep faster.
- How to detect and relieve food allergies.
- A tip for preventing car sickness.
- How to prevent bladder infections.
- A vitamin that may repel insects when taken orally.
- A simple technique to relieve tension.
- How to relieve dry skin.
- 4 tips to avoid food poisoning.
- How to stop snoring.
- 3 ways to avoid stomach irritation when taking aspirin.
- 4 vitamins that may be harmful if taken in excess.
- 6 aids to eliminate constipation.
- 7 suggestions to relieve heartburn.
- A safe, simple home treatment for sore, tired feet.
- How to relieve bloating and puffiness.
- A common food to reduce cholesterol.
- 10 tips to ease back pain.
- Latest research findings on the good effects of vitamins, minerals and other nutrients.

D You can order the book direct from the publisher and save. To order simply send £12.95 *(which includes postage and handling),* together with your name, address and book title to: Carnell Ltd, Dept.   , Alresford, nr. Colchester, Essex CO7 8AP. You can return the book within 30 days for a full refund if not satisfied.

ranging, i.e. foot odour and cellulite (again, to keep all the readers interested), and the cumulative effect is such that you feel that the book is absolutely packed with information.

D The last paragraph adds another benefit/desire, by telling the customer that they can order the book direct and *save money*. The rest of the response paragraph is absolutely standard.

This very simple advert has successfully sold tens of thousands of books.

Straight prose – Government Auction Handbook

A The headline indicates that the reader will be able to get a bargain and therefore appeals to another basic human instinct – making and saving money. 'Handbook' is an nice, easy-going sort of word – it doesn't make the auction sound like hard work; 'Manual' would have seemed rather more heavy going and thus off-putting.

B The first paragraph addresses the reader directly and engages their attention with a question.

C The second paragraph confirms the implication of the title – that the biggest benefit of this book is that there are fantastic bargains to be had.

D The third paragraph makes use of the specific, i.e. 10%, boats, planes etc., to further illustrate the point just made and fire the imagination. By now the reader is already in his speedboat crashing through the surf! This paragraph also counters a possible objection by adding that the goods are in first-class condition, despite the discounted price.

E The table of examples is perhaps one of the most effective devices in the entire advert; by giving real-life examples of bargains found it shows not only how much money can be saved, but also that there is something for everyone at auction.

A

GOVERNMENT AUCTION HANDBOOK

NEW 1993 EDITION

B Ever wondered what happens to the stock and assets of a company when declared bankrupt? Ever considered where the property and possessions seized by HM Customs and Excise are sold? Ever questioned what the Official Receiver, Liquidators, Bailiffs, and the Collector of Taxes do with the goods they sequestrate?

C They're all sold off at auction to the highest bidder. Various government departments enter goods for sale at these auctions – *sometimes with no reserve prices!* The goods offered at these auctions have to be sold there and then for whatever they will fetch.

D Most items realise no more than 10% of their market value. You will find all manner of goods there, including boats, planes, automobiles, office equipment, jewellery, video cameras, televisions, fine art and much, much more. And all at knockdown prices. Just take a look at the examples below, noted at recent auctions, all either brand new or in first class condition.

Item	Retail £	Auction £
VW Golf GTI, E reg	5,000	1,000
Phillips Car CD Player	350	59
Jaguar XJS, G reg	16,000	7,800
Apple Laptop Computer	1,500	60
Engine Tuner	350	40
Mita Photocopier	490	18
Renault 21 Turbo	8,000	4,500
Honda Moped	175	46
Fax Machine	1,435	150
Headlamp Beam Setter	150	8
Puch 5 Speed Racing Bike	100	14
Carbon Fibre Fishing Tackle	180	10
Compressor	350	150
Maestro Van, B reg	900	275
Case of Wine	50	5
Citroen GS Palas	300	80
Colour Television	200	40
Ford Escort Van	2,950	1,700
Trailer	300	40
Garage Rolling Road	70,000	10,000
Dishwasher	250	15

E

These auctions are held throughout the country practically every day of the week. The only reason you may not have heard about them is simply because they are not widely publicised. Contrary to popular belief, these auctions are NOT a closed shop exclusively reserved for traders - anyone is allowed to attend them.

F **The Government Auction Handbook** provides you with a comprehensive list of auctions throughout the country - their sale days and times. Also included with your handbook are instructions on how to pay the lowest possible price and how to set yourself up as a dealer, simply and easily. But this is not one of those books professing to tell you how to get rich quick. It's primarily designed to *save* you money, lots of money.

G As one reader in Norfolk puts it in a recent letter to us: 'Your book was the best £12 I have ever spent'. And another reader, this time in Yorkshire, writes to say: 'I have made enough profit from ONE sale to pay for the Handbook 90 times over!'

H If you're the kind of person who would like a brand new Sony CD HI-FI for fifteen quid, an IBM computer system for as little as a tenner, a speedboat with 40 horse power outboard for less than the cost of a romantic weekend in Grimsby, or a car for ten pence on the pound, then you really should send off for **The Government Auction Handbook** immediately. Just complete and return the form below.

© 1992 Carnell Ltd., 37 Salisbury House, London Wall, London EC2M 5PJ

I

To: Carnell Ltd., Alresford nr. Colchester, Essex CO7 8AP.
Please rush me _____ copies of **The Government Auction Handbook** at £12.95 each (includes p&p) on the understanding that if not delighted I can return it within 30 days for a full refund.

☐ I enclose my cheque for £_____ (Payable to Carnell Ltd)
☐ Please charge my credit card no:

Account No. ☐☐☐☐☐☐☐☐☐☐☐☐☐☐☐☐ (Visa/Access)

Name _____ BLOCK

Address _____ CAPITALS

_____ Postcode_____ PLEASE

Signed_____ Date_____

Please allow up to 21 days for delivery. We hope to be able to make a variety of further interesting offers from reputable companies - if you prefer not to receive such offers please write to Carnell Ltd. at the above address.

Registered in England No. 2470149

F The next two paragraphs counter more possible objections and keep the maximum number of people interested by emphasising that the auctions are held frequently, all around the UK and are open to anyone, not just dealers. It then lists more benefits, i.e. that it is easy to be successful at auction with the help of the book, even to set up in business. But it sensibly stops short of exaggeration by stipulating that the book does not promise instant wealth and is designed more to save money. This greatly adds to the credibility of the other claims.

G The next paragraph makes use of a customer quote – 'Your book was the best £12 I have ever spent', again adding to the credibility of the examples given previously.

H The last paragraph summarises the benefits to the customer, and by using tempting examples, confirms the desire of the reader.

I The coupon is absolutely standard.

This advert did nothing more than make use of the copy-writing rules given above and it sold almost 200,000 copies of the book at £12.95 per copy – about £2.5 million of revenue. Of course the product was a very good one, but the advert undoubtedly helped; it had impact, pace and a momentum that quite swept the customer along to the 'action' stage. It did what a good advertisement should do.

A WORD ABOUT CREATIVE AGENCIES

You can, of course, employ an agency to write your copy. Many people do this and it can work very successfully. The *BRAD Advertiser and Agency List* has a comprehensive section on creative and design agencies – addresses, telephone numbers etc. But bear in mind the importance of knowing your product. You are probably the best-qualified person to write about this item that you know and like. Don't be surprised if other people lack quite the same enthusiasm and attitude. Having said that, there are some extremely talented copy-writers about and it is just possible that they will come up with an angle that makes the campaign run. This rarely comes cheap. But sometimes you have to speculate to accumulate!

Having said that, many mail order operators manage successfully without outside help. David Kerley, Commercial Director of Unwins Seeds Ltd, has always maintained that the key is to 'get the offer right'. That is to say, if you are offering the right product at the right price you can easily produce your own advertisement. In his experience, 80 per cent of an advert's effectiveness lies in the offer, and only 20 per cent in the creative side.

8

ADVERTISEMENTS: THE PRACTICAL DETAILS

WE HAVE just discussed the general layout of your advertisement – the headline, body copy and response mechanism. Now you have to decide upon the fine details of presentation and design, where best to place your ad . . . and how.

CREATING ARTWORK FOR YOUR ADVERTISEMENT

The most important elements of design are as follows.

The general size of your advertisement

This is sometimes governed by your product. An advert for flower seeds might well be shorter and less complex than one for a sophisticated piece of electrical equipment. An expensive product will normally need more space to convince the reader to buy than would a £10 item. But, whatever your message, it should be contained within the ad as tightly as possible. Space costs money. So don't waste it. The advertisement opposite is a good example of a relatively short advert, which none the less says everything and is selling a higher priced item.

Certainly in the early stages of your business you should always aim for the smallest/cheapest space possible. As you gain in success and confidence you can move to larger ads. But always remember that unless you are making money (see Chapter 11), even the smallest ad is too expensive.

The actual measurements of your advertisement

These will vary, depending upon the paper or magazine.

Newspapers

Newspapers work in 'column space', i.e. the width of the ad is measured by columns, the depth in centimetres. A '20 × 2' would refer to an ad that was 20 cm deep and 2 columns wide (depth is always given first). Another common size is a '25 × 4', i.e. 25 cm deep and 4 columns wide. One size that is effective is a single-column 'strip ad' (shown on page 122 split in two columns); not only is it economical, but has the advantage of looking 'newsy' and seems to catch the eye.

These are standard sizes used throughout the industry and only differ from paper to paper in the width measurement of the column. It makes sense to use these standard spaces whenever possible:

- because you will only need one or two pieces of artwork made up wherever you choose to advertise;
- because these 'classic spaces' are easier for the paper to work around (remember that they have to plan each page exactly so that there isn't even a cm of blank space) and are the ones they most want to sell.

The best advertising rates are always given to people booking standard size measurements.

Observer Offer

Outdoor Games for all the family –

A set of Boules for £26.95 and
a choice of Croquet Sets from £65.95
Prices include p&p

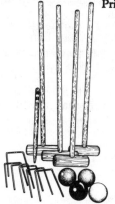 

Boules is an easy and fun game to play in the garden, on the beach or on gravel. Our set of Boule comprises 4 brilliantly polished silver coloured balls made from steel alloy measuring 73mm in diameter and 640 grammes in weight plus one Jack packed in a neat vinyl carry case. We have two styles of Croquet sets; the Full Size at £95.95 is the professionals croquet set and comprises 4 hardwood mallets 37 inches long with 2¾ inch diameter heads, 4 full size 3⅝ inch diameter balls, 6 hoops made from iron coated with white nylon, a winning peg and rules all stored in a strong box with wooden ends and rope handles. The Garden Croquet set is £65.95 and designed to introduce people to the game. It has 4 hardwood mallets 37 inches long with 2⅜ inch diameter heads, 4 full size balls, 6 galvanised iron hoops, a winning peg and rules all stored in a sturdy cardboard box. If you are not satisfied please return within 7 days for a refund.

For Access/Visa orders please call 0536 420667

DESIGNER CLOTHES AT GIVEAWAY PRICES

A new book reveals how and where to buy designer clothes at up to 75% discount. This book is of vital importance to everyone interested in presenting themselves in the very best light at all times without having to spend a fortune. Here are a few of the tips covered in this *Designer Clothes Discount Guide*:

- Where to find original samples, including designs which were never sold to the general public and which are quietly sold off at cost prices.
- How to get cancelled and returned orders of designer clothes at steep discounts.
- What to look for when buying overcuts, which go at whatever price they will fetch.
- What to look for in seconds, some of which have nothing more than a drawn thread or a few missed stitches and then only apparent on close inspection.
- How and where to find surplus fabric at a fraction of their original cost.
- How to get on a top designer's mailing list for end of season sales.
- 24 'permanent' sales shops where you can buy top designer clothes at large discounts all through the year.
- 4 important group sales events where you can purchase designer clothes at wholesale prices or less.
- 10 places handling designer fabrics at steep discounts.
- Where to buy Karl Lagerfeld, Ungaro, Gianni Versace, Giorgio Armani, Byblos, Valentino, Gucci, Christian Lacroix, Miyake, Ralph Lauren, Christian Dior, Frank Usher, Arabella Pollen, John Galliano and many, many other top designer clothes for less cost than you could ever imagine.

Get all the facts. Order *The Designer Clothes Discount Guide* today direct from the publisher and save. To order send name, address and the book title together with £12.95 (*includes handling and despatch*) to Carnell Ltd., Dept , Alresford, nr Colchester, Essex CO7 8AP. You can return the book within 30 days for a full refund if not completely satisfied.

THE NATIONAL NEWSPAPER
MOPS
MAIL ORDER PROTECTION SCHEME

An example of an effective Carnell single-column 'strip ad', shown here split over two columns.

Magazines

Magazines also work to standard sizes. Most magazines are A4 size, with the text measuring approximately 270 mm deep × 189 mm wide. This is then divided in half, quarters, eighths etc. for smaller ads. These measurements vary slightly, depending upon the particular magazine. Whether you are advertising in a paper or magazine, always check the exact measurements required, in cm and mm. You will then know how much space you have to play with and can avoid needless typesetting corrections.

Choosing a typeface

When selecting a typeface the principle to follow is very simple. When reading papers people have a relatively short concentration span. If they have to struggle with words that are too small or unclear, they will give up. Use a crisp, sharp typeface and print that is large enough to be read by the average eye; it is a good idea to use the same typeface and typesize as the paper you are advertising in. After all, they have researched what is best for the reader, so why try to be clever and do something different?

You also want to use bold lettering or italics for emphasis and special effect. Bold letters are best left for the headline and important details in the response mechanism, such as your address and company name (see page 124). Italics are usually reserved for emphasis within the body copy – to heighten the unique selling point (USP) or to reiterate the benefits. But don't clutter up the ad – if your copy is well written you won't need many props.

Pictures and illustrations

Depending upon your product, a picture/illustration may or may not be useful. In the book business, the product is best described by its contents, not by the proverbial cover, and therefore pictures of the product are rarely used. If, however,

Marshalls **FEN BRED SEEDS**

The Experts' Choice

GIANT FEN GLOBE ONION SETS

Gardeners who know their onions insist on Giant Fen Globe and now's the time to order to secure delivery for April planting.

Exclusive to Marshalls, Giant Fen Globe is the most consistently successful onion from sets ever bred — notching up two RHS Awards and building up a faithful following in the kitchen and on the showbench for over 30 years.

These unique onion sets are given a special heat treatment to prevent bolting. Unlike other varieties which produce flattish onions resulting in a high degree of kitchen wastage, Giant Fen Globe produces a huge crop of perfectly round onions with a deliciously mild flavour.

Often 30lbs or more can be grown from each bag, and they will usually keep until the following May.

Small wonder many gardeners will grow no other onion.

S.E. Marshall & Co Ltd, Wisbech, Cambridgeshire PE13 2RF. Company regd in England No 569255.

1 bag – £1.45 (POSTAGE & PACKING FREE)
2-4 bags – £1.29 per bag
5 bags or more – £1.15 per bag

ORDER WHILE STOCKS LAST

To: S.E. Marshall & Co Ltd, Box   , Wisbech, Cambridgeshire PE13 2RF.

Please send me_____(qty) bags of GIANT FEN GLOBE ONION SETS.

I enclose cheque/postal order for a total of £_____(including P&P).

Name_____

Address_____

_____

_____Post Code_____

Delivery will commence in mid-March and continue until early April – the correct time for planting.

MARSHALLS SEEDS
A must for vegetable growers

☎ **day or night**
Wisbech (0945) 583407

This advertisement makes good use of typography and includes an effective photograph.

you are selling gadgets, food, crafts or clothes – things where the visual appearance reinforces the benefits of the product, you might usefully include a picture. Space restrictions mean that it will have to be fairly small and therefore clear. A good black and white photo or a line-drawing will be acceptable (see opposite and page 126). Don't even consider the possibility of full colour adverts until you are confident about the finances of your business. But always think carefully before using pictures. They will increase the space needed and push up your advertising costs. Only use them if you cannot find a better way with words.

Preparing finished artwork

Almost all media require you to produce 'camera-ready' artwork. This means that your advertisement must be professionally typeset and produced as a bromide (a photographic image of your artwork – a black image on white paper) so that the quality and definition is in line with the rest of the paper/magazine. This is one area where you must use the services of a professional, in this case, a typesetter or printer. You will have no difficulty finding one, just use your local *Yellow Pages*.

Show them your ad – handwritten at this stage, and specify the size of the ad (in mm), typeface, typesize, bold/italic parts etc. It will probably take them a day or two to do and you must then check it to make sure that everything is correct, especially the details of your response mechanism. Most typesetters charge from about £10 plus per hour and about £10–£15 per bromide (costs can be significantly lower outside London). So keep mistakes to a minimum! Lastly, ask them to keep the typesetting on disk/file, so that you can make necessary alterations later on at a nominal cost.

Two Dwarf Lilacs -

only £19.95
incl. p&p

In May and June there is nothing to compare with the delicious fragrance of lilacs. Most lilacs grow to large shrubs, but the ones on offer today are miniatures, one white, one blue and are ideal for small gardens where they should grow to no more than 4½ feet tall. These lilac bushes will thrive in a sunny position, or even in partial shade and are ideal for growing in 12 inch (or wider) tubs or planters on a patio. The lilacs will arrive with full growing instructions and are on offer for only £19.95 for two including postage and packing.

If you are not satisfied please return within 7 days for a refund.

For Access/Visa orders please phone 0536 420667

— — — — — — — please cut — — — — — — —

I wish to order.................**sets of Dwarf Lilac(s) at £19.95** (incl P&P).

I enclose crossed cheque value £............ payable to *Observer Offers.*

I wish to pay by Access/Visa Card number

Signature...Expiry Date...........................

UK readers only. Subject to availability.   Allow 28 days for delivery.

Send to: **Observer Dwarf Lilacs, 88 Station Road, Burton Latimer, Northants NN15 5JW**

Name...

Address..

.... Postcode................................

If you do not wish to receive details of other offers or services please tick this box ☐

PLACING YOUR ADVERTISEMENT IN THE MEDIA

You might have the best advert in the world but if you can't place it in the right media at the right price and at the right time, you won't make money. There are several issues to consider.

Which media to use

In Chapters 1 and 3 we looked at identifying your potential customers and your product. You now have to choose the media which are most likely to match the customers to the product. And, according to *BRAD*, there are over 9,000 papers and magazines in the UK. So you have quite a choice! The broad categories are as follows:

- national press;
- regional press;
- national magazines (which will be either consumer and special interest publications or business and professional publications).

In order to match these up with your customers you need to find out whether your media will:

- have an upper, middle or mass market bias;
- have a distinct male/female readership;
- be read by a particular age group.

You will find this information most important when targeting national and regional newspapers. National magazines have a more obvious reader profile and the reader's particular interest is often reflected in the magazine title, e.g. *Car Magazine*, *The Angler*, *House and Garden*. National newspapers have slightly more subtle variations of reader profile, which you must understand clearly in order to place successful ads. Sometimes your

desired customer profile will be very obvious, i.e. you would
expect a book on football to be male orientated. Sometimes it
will be more general, for example, a book on making money.
Either way, you still need to understand what type of people
read each paper to decide where your ad is most likely to do
well, even if that turns out to be almost anywhere – as I suspect
would a book about money!

Listed below are all the major national papers and their
various characteristics.

Name of paper	Circulation	Upper/middle/ mass market bias	Male/Female	Age
Daily Telegraph	1,037,375	Upper	c. 53% male	} slightly older
Sunday Telegraph	583,831	Upper	c. 52% male	
Times	376,836	Upper	50/50	average
Sunday Times	1,202,787	Upper	50/50	slightly younger
Financial Times	289,446	Upper	male	slightly older
Observer	537,216	Upper	50/50	average
Guardian	420,154	Upper	50/50	slightly younger
Independent	362,099	Upper	50/50	slightly younger
Independent on Sunday	407,771	Upper	50/50	slightly younger
Today	538,418	Middle	50/50	slightly younger
Daily Mail	1,751,650	Middle	50/50	average
Mail on Sunday	2,070,894	Middle	50/50	slightly younger
Daily Express	1,507,087	Middle	50/50	average
Sunday Express	1,727,957	Middle	50/50	slightly older
Sun	3,545,337	Mass	53% male	slightly younger
News of the World	4,692,341	Mass	50/50	slightly older
Daily Star	788,674	Mass	53% male	
Daily Sport	280,000	Mass	male	} average
Daily Mirror	2,722,779	Mass	50/50	
Sunday Mirror	2,671,198	Mass	50/50	
Sunday People	2,062,000	Mass	50/50	slightly older

(Circulation figures taken from the May 1993 copy of BRAD)

BRAD
All media – national, regional, papers and magazines – are listed
in *BRAD* (which stands for *British Rate and Data*), published

monthly, which gives a complete profile on each title (see the back of this book). Among other things it lists the title of each publication, details of the publisher, circulation, cost of advertisements, contact names etc. It groups some media by subject matter – very useful when you have a specialist product to sell.

Circulation figures

BRAD also lists the circulation of each paper/magazine. This is an important piece of information and is worth looking into in more detail. If the initials VFD (Verified Free Distribution) appear next to the circulation figure this means that the paper is a free one. Being free can make it harder for you to determine whether or not your ad is being seen by the right people. So do look out for that. If the paper has the initials ABC after it, this means that paper is bought on the newstands and that its circulation has been checked by the Audit Bureau of Circulation.

Do not confuse circulation with readership. Circulation means the number of people who have bought the paper/ magazine. Readership means the number of people who get to handle each copy. A daily paper has a 2.4 – 3-person readership, while a copy of *Reader's Digest*, often left lying around in dentists' waiting rooms, might have a 20-person readership. Always base your calculations on circulation, never on the more nebulous readership figures.

WHERE TO START

Generally speaking, in the first stages of advertising your product you should stick closely to the media most likely to be read by your potential customers. This is often, but not always, one of the middle or upper market papers; remember that mail order products are purchased with disposable income and you will understand why. Obviously this readership profile is always going to be something of a generalisation; it is true that the *Sun* and *News of the World* are essentially mass market papers, but they are also read by sections of the upper market. It is simply that their bias is towards the mass market.

So, if your product has general appeal, start by advertising in 'upper market' papers such as the *Independent* or *Guardian*, then move to middle market and finally to mass market. When advertising a new book we often start by running an ad in these papers; it seems to give a good readout of how popular the product is likely to be. You will find that unless your product is intended specifically for the mass market, this will be the hardest area to crack. Occasionally something comes along with such wide appeal that you can advertise almost anywhere and make money. But most of the time you will have to start at the 'top' of the market and work downwards.

Products with a narrow target market, for example, a piece of photography equipment, tend to sell well in more specific media, often specialist magazines. Here you know exactly what you are getting because the reader profile is so well defined.

Companies such as Unwins Seeds and Lakeland Plastics have carefully refined their choice of media (and of particular pages within the media) to target the people most likely to buy their products. It would not be sufficient, for instance, for Unwins simply to place an advert at random in a national newspaper – it has to be the gardening page. Alternatively, they use specialist gardening magazines. Lakeland Plastics concentrate exclusively on food and catering magazines, since adverts in the nationals would reach too wide and ill-defined an audience.

You should also get into the habit of looking at where similar products to yours are being advertised. If the same ad appears regularly in one place, it is a fair indication that the choice of media is a good one. For further inspiration, look at the 'National Advertisers' section of the *BRAD Advertiser and Agency List*; it shows you who advertises what – and where.

Cost/1,000

You should then compare the cost per 1,000 readers, to gauge which of your potential papers/magazines is going to give you the best deal. For instance, if you were offered an ad at £300, for a paper with a circulation of 300,000, the cost would work out at £1 per 1,000 readers. This would actually be a better deal than a paper with a higher circulation of 600,000, but charging £900 or £1.50 per 1,000.

But understand that this only applies if both media offer an equally good reader profile. If the £900 ad was read by more women and that was your target market, you might be better off paying the extra 50p per 1,000. So remember that the cost per 1,000 comparison is only really effective between papers that you feel will work equally well for your product.

WHICH SECTION OF THE MEDIA TO USE

Within the media in general

Generally speaking, your advertisement will run in one of two places within the various media.

Classified

In the classified section your advert would appear on a page covered with other (often smaller sized) adverts, usually towards the back of the paper/magazine. There is no editorial at all on this page. Classified positions are usually cheaper than display because you are further back in the paper and there is a greater chance of your particular ad being lost on the page – although it is often divided into sections, such as gardening, gifts etc. Having said that, it sometimes happens that a classified ad draws good response, precisely because anyone looking for, say, a gardening product, will know where to look for it.

Display

If you book a display position, your ad will appear within the main pages of the paper, surrounded by editorial; this is generally agreed to be the better choice. The ad gets noticed more easily and the effect is less cramped than with a classified space. You can request a 'solus' position on the page, but unless you are paying extra this will not be guaranteed. Your advertisement will also probably be inserted towards the front of the paper – this is a definite plus point; after all, people do buy the paper to read the news and there is always a possibility that having done that they will throw the paper away without even noticing your ad if it is languishing towards the back pages! You can also specify sections you definitely do not want to go into, such as the sport/business pages, traditionally less successful areas for most consumer products. But always think first of the product and where it will sit most comfortably. An ad for sportswear would obviously stand the best chance of success on the sports pages.

Within the page

Newspaper advertisements are almost always run on the bottom half of the page (not true of magazines), mainly because the top of the page catches the eye more easily and is therefore reserved for news items. The top right-hand corner of the page is always cited as the very best place to be.

So, failing that, the second-best place you can be is bottom right, then bottom left and lastly, stuck in the middle! On top of all this, the right-hand page is always thought better than the left, again, because it draws the eye. Positioning is important – it is there to be negotiated and to avoid paying for if possible. As you will see later, price can be everything. Buying cheap is the key to making money.

One thing you must request is that there is no advertisement on the other side of the page, whose coupon backs on to your ad; because if someone cuts out the other coupon, the return from your ad can be weakened by anything up to 10 per cent.

Newspaper reader offers

While considering different media and where to advertise product, it is worth taking a look at newspaper reader offers. From the outside they look very much like any other 'cash off the page' mail order ad. But, whereas the products are being advertised at the newspaper's expense, the product is actually supplied and fulfilled by an outside operator. The advantage to the supplier is that they get national newspaper coverage without having to pay for the adverts. In return, the paper takes a percentage commission of the supplier's turnover on that ad. If the volume of response is sufficient this can work well for both parties.

But don't all rush, thinking that this answers the problem of raising advertising capital. National newspapers will normally only deal with a large and established operator; they have to be certain that you have the stock and the experience to deliver. Failing that, you might have better luck approaching regional newspapers or specialist magazines, who might be somewhat more flexible and better suited to the capacity of your operation. It is always worth your while asking.

TESTING

Most important of all, it is essential to test your proposition. It will save you lots of money and heartache. The reason for testing is to discover whether or not your product is actually going to appeal to the customer and how best to word the ad to achieve maximum response. Obviously you want to know this before you commit thousands of pounds to advertising.

Whenever possible you should limit your risk by testing as cheaply as possible. Most of the time your advertisements will be in the display sections of the media. But for the purposes of testing you could run a small classified ad, which can be very cost effective. This is essentially just a few lines of text containing the essence of the larger, display ad. It comprises all the same elements – headline, benefits, request for the sale etc., but it does so in just a few words, which costs you tens of pounds rather than hundreds. Typical classified ads might read as follows:

1. **Mammoth vegetables!** Exciting giant vegetable seed selection – pumpkin, marrow, onion and leek.
Don't delay, send £5 to Smithco Ltd, 37 Jones St, London, SW2 1AP.

2.

> ## EARN £180 A DAY AS A WRITER
> This eye-opening report by the Editor of one of the leading magazines for writers will show you how to write successfully for publication and profit. Send £2.50 to: Weavers Press Publishing (WW) Tregeraint House, Zennor, St Ives, Cornwall, TR2 3DB.

Classifieds are very useful indicators of product success. If your offer works in classifieds, it will almost certainly work in display.

However, classifieds have certain disadvantages.

- They are only really useful for cheaper products. People are rarely prepared to send more than £10 (absolute maximum) in response to a three-line ad, unless you go to the trouble of first sending further free details and then asking for the sale.

- You are limited by the fact that only a few papers have good classified sections; the *Sunday Times* and the *Daily Telegraph* do, but they are geared towards recruitment. The *News of the World*, *Sun*, *Mirror* and *Sunday Mirror* have semi-classified sections called Postal Bargains/Buy By Post etc.; you could test your proposition here, but only if the paper is suitable for your target market.
- You lose much of your potential audience, because classified sections tend to be read only by people with a specific interest and are often ignored by the casual reader.

The bottom line is that you can test with a classified ad if the product is a low price one and the publication is relevant to your target market. Otherwise, you would be better off testing with your full-size ad in display.

Begin by running your display ad in just one place. If it fails, run exactly the same ad somewhere else to see if your choice of media was responsible. If that also fails, start testing elements within the ad. The secret of testing is to test only one thing at a time. That is to say, if you think your ad has failed to bring in good response because the headline and body copy were wrong, test the ad in the same paper, preferably on the same day of the week, but just change the headline. If the ad then works, you will know why. If it doesn't work, then test again, this time changing the body copy. Accurate comparisons (right down to the same place on the page if possible) are crucial if you are to isolate the reasons for the success/failure of your advertisement. The science of mail order is never more apparent than here. Discipline yourself to test properly.

Of course you have to know when to stop. Assuming that your resources are finite, you should test maybe two or three things – first the headline, then the body copy and possibly the response mechanism – before giving up on the ad. The bottom line is that if there were a real demand for your product, it would somehow manifest itself. One of the great strengths of mail order is that you can run very simple ads and get a very honest response. If the customer doesn't rate the product he or she simply won't send off for it! Remember that the volume of mail is the best indicator of product success/failure.

Lastly, you could always test the market reaction to a new product free of charge by getting mentions and write-ups in the media. The Tin Pot Company, who sell hand-painted watering cans by mail order, have managed to build their business despite *never* having paid for an advert. Jill and David Redbourn Miller very enterprisingly went through BRAD and sent a letter to every home interest and gardening magazine (see opposite). Approximately 20 per cent of the media approached ran a piece on how to buy the watering cans. Apart from being an extraordinary success rate, it allowed the Redbourn Millers to experiment free of charge and find out what price, colour, size etc sold best. Now the media approach *them* for new products.

Don't forget – newspapers and magazines always need new and interesting copy. You could do very well by simply supplying that demand.

WHEN TO ADVERTISE

The mail order market is very much a seasonal one. Almost regardless of the product, there are certain times of the year which are much better for advertising. There are, of course, products which prove an exception to this rule, but generally speaking, there are three periods of the year when it is best to advertise.

January to the end of March

You may be quite surprised to read this, but people do often hold back a little money for after Christmas (traditionally for sale shopping), and they often feel the need to treat themselves in the dark and cold weeks that follow the festive season. Given

THE TIN POT COMPANY
51, Thayers Farm Road
Beckenham
Kent BR3 4LY
Tel: 081-658 3471

Dear Madam –

We seek to introduce ourselves as the manufacturers of the unique range of "TIN POT" watering cans. Each one is individually hand painted and they are equally suitable for indoor and outdoor gardeners alike.

We are actively engaged in distribution by way of Direct Mail Order which enables us to maintain our exceedingly competitive price structure. This you can see from the enclosed illustrated Leaflet which accompanies our Price List/Order Form. These we send, free of charge, to each enquiry generated.

We feel our product is sufficiently original and attractive to be of interest to your readers and is, therefore, worthy of a mention in your "SHOPFRONT" column. We hope you agree!

We look forward expectantly to your favourable reaction and would be happy to supply samples for photography, prints or transparencies and copy such as may be required.

Yours sincerely,

DAVID REDBOURN MILLER.

David & Jill Redbourn Miller.
V.A.T. Reg. No 574 3411 45

that the weather is usually bad, people also spend much more time at home, some of it reading the papers more thoroughly and more often than they might otherwise do (newspaper sales are at their peak at this time of year). As a result of all this they respond more positively and more frequently to mail order advertisements. It makes common sense really: it's a cold, dark and wet January day. You may need to buy something but just cannot get motivated to go out and brave the elements. It's much easier to fill in a coupon, pop it in an envelope and post it next time you go out. *Voilà*. A mail order sale.

September to November

This is also a good time of year to advertise mail order products, particularly gifts suitable for Christmas. By September, children have started going back to school, parents have a bit more time on their hands and, albeit reluctantly, their thoughts turn to the next big calendar event – Christmas! As we all know, planning for this holiday starts as early as October, and this is when most mail order Christmas items are purchased. November is also busy, but most people are aware that postal items take up to 30 days for delivery, and they don't want to risk not receiving the item in time to give it for Christmas. So, by mid-November, your orders will start to tail off a little. There are one or two seasonal industries that get busy at this time of year too; September and October are the traditional months for ordering seeds by post and most mail order gardening business is carried out between September and February.

April to June

This is very much an 'in between' time for advertising and your success will depend very much upon the product and the weather! April and May can often be cold and wet (snow in April is not unknown), which is of course every mail order person's delight. And it is a good time of year to sell, for example, garden furniture or any item connected to outdoor pursuits and the warmer summer months. If, however, the weather is wonderful, you will immediately lose much of your potential audience. So be guided by what's happening around you and by the elements.

WHEN NOT TO ADVERTISE

There are just a few golden rules here. It is usually a bad idea to advertise at the following times.

From July until the end of August

This is traditionally our holiday time. The children are off school, the weather is at its best (well, a little bit of optimism doesn't hurt!) and many families go away for a break. Newspaper circulation goes right down at this time of year. People cancel their subscription while they are away; they are too busy out in the sun to wade through a paper and, even if they do, the chances are that they will be feeling too relaxed to bother with filling in and cutting out coupons. It's just too much effort.

In December

A good time for shops but bad for mail order.

Given that you are asking the customer to wait an average of 21 days for their goods, it is simply too late to order for Christmas. People do not respond well to mail order at this time of year.

During any public holiday

Easter, Christmas, Whitsun and bank holidays; again, people either go away or get together with family and can be too busy eating, talking, arguing and sleeping to bother with

advertisements. Moreover, commuter sales form a large proportion of all newspaper sales – so when people are not
commuting they are also not buying newspapers.

When economics, politics or the weather disrupt normal routine

It is important to understand how seemingly unconnected
events can influence your mail order response. I said earlier that
bad weather was actually good as it keeps the customer at home
in front of the fire. But equally, if the weather is really bad, such
as snowstorms, newspaper delivery is affected. That means that
newspapers don't reach the shops from the printing works and,
even if they do, many people cannot get to the shops to buy
them, nor can newspaper deliverers get out!

World economics and politics also take their toll. A sudden
outbreak of war, e.g. the Gulf War, or political instability, e.g.
the downfall of Margaret Thatcher, can each create uncertainty
among the public, and they hesitate to buy until order and confidence have been restored. Many people also feel that it is in-
appropriate to do something as frivolous as ordering luxury
goods through the post when there is war being waged, especially if their own country is involved. There was a significant
downturn in our own business on both of the occasions just
mentioned above.

Similarly, you may be the victim of an untimely news story.
Anything criticising a product or area close to your business
could have damaging consequences. Edwina Currie's
comments on eggs is an obvious example. There is nothing
much you can do about this or indeed any of the other examples
given above, but you must build into your business forecast an
allowance for these setbacks.

HOW TO PLACE AN ADVERTISEMENT

There are two possible ways to place ads in the news and magazine media.

Via a media independent

This is an individual or business which exists simply to place advertising for other people's products. They work on the basis of negotiating a significant discount on the rate card (the 'official' rates of advertising issued by the individual media). Some of this is retained as their own fee and the rest is passed on to you, the client. The media buyer can command good discounts partly because of the volume of business it gives to the paper and also through its experience of dealing in this specific area. Equally, the media are happy to deal with the buyer because they can be sure of selling their quota of advertising space and know that they will get paid on time. You, the client, can also be confident of using media independents; first, because they are more knowledgeable than you and, second, because they are regulated by the industry 'governing' bodies (the Newspaper Publishers' Association Ltd, the Periodical Publishers' Association and the Newspaper Society). They also have to prove their solvency, have paid-up share capital of at least £50,000 and provide annual audited accounts for inspection.

The level of discount negotiated will vary from buyer to buyer, as will their fees. Generally speaking, a media buyer can command discounts of up to 75 per cent (sometimes more) on rate card; 60 per cent of this is negotiated and the last 15 per cent is given specifically because they are a professional media buyer. This all amounts to an enormous saving that dramatically improves your chances of making money from the ad. Depending upon how much business you give them, the

buyer's fees will be between 4–7 per cent of the final 15 per cent
discount. For example:

	£	cost of ad – running total £s
1. Rate card	1,000	1,000
2. 60% discount	(600)	400
3. Extra 15% discount on £400	(60)	340
4. 10%, i.e. £40 is passed on to you and 5% i.e. £20 is held back as the media buyer's fee	20	**360**

In other words, an ad that 'officially' costs £1,000 has cost you
just £360.

The downside is that a media independent, especially a large
one, will normally only handle a client giving them £100k+
worth of bookings per annum. But many companies do take
first-timers and it is well worth looking around for a good one;
81 per cent of national newspaper mail order advertisers, from
sole traders up to the large companies, are represented by media
buyers. The *BRAD Advertiser and Agency List* publishes a
comprehensive list of media independents and ad agencies. If
they have the initials NPA, NS, PPA under their listing it is an
indication that the agency handles mail order accounts. You can
also contact the Association of Media Independents (address at
the back of the book). Founded in 1981, it comprises independent companies that specialise in the planning, buying and
evaluation of advertising. Its members take on both large and
small advertising budgets. You can ask for their brochure
which lists member companies.

Remember that in this situation you are the unknown quantity and they may well insist that you pay up front until your
creditworthiness is established. Other points to remember are

that media buyers only buy space. They do not check or produce copy (as distinct from ad agencies, who do all that for you but may charge up to 15 per cent, rather than 5 per cent, for the privilege). That is up to you. Nor will they ensure that your ad is coded. That is also up to you, or the newspaper, if they have agreed to put the code in themselves. What they will do is provide you with a report sheet variously called a 'media amendment report'/regular report/media schedule, usually faxed through on the day of booking, which will give you the day, date, cost and size of the ad and where it has been placed. This allows you to:

- make a diary note to buy the paper concerned;
- note the cost etc. in your order book;
- make up analysis sheets, ready to write up the results (see Chapter 11);
- alert the fulfilment house/whoever is packaging the goods to watch out for orders after the advert has appeared.

Yourself

You are more likely to place your own advertisements in the early stages of the business. That is, when you are only placing a few at a time and want to keep costs down. The key point to remember is that even though you may not have the experience or the muscle of the big media buyers, you are still offering your custom/money to the media, and can therefore negotiate the rates.

The procedure is quite simple, although it may appear a little daunting at first. Find out the telephone number of the paper/magazine you wish to deal with. Call and ask to be sent the published rate card; then you have an idea of the normal rates charged. When you are familiar with the rates, call again. Ask to be put through to the advertising department, classified or display (whichever you have chosen). Deal with just one particular person at the other end of the line. Try not to let them know that you are new to this; simply tell them what it is you are selling (offer to show them your ad), the size of ad you want and when you want it to run. There is no need to be aggressive or pushy. Just try to sound relaxed and confident – and start to negotiate. Remember one thing – no one pays rate card! Ask for their best deal on the space and in any case aim to pay no more than 50 per cent of rate card and if possible, one-third.

Buying advertising space is really just a game – but you must play by the rules. The person selling the space is used to being asked for a discount (they may have already built it into their rates!), so don't be embarrassed to ask. Your profit margin depends upon it. Aim to build up an ongoing relationship with that person. Let them know:

- how much you are generally prepared to pay;
- that they can call you at the last minute if they have unsold space;
- that you are flexible as to where your ad is positioned in the paper (within reason).

You will be very popular with the beleaguered advertising executive, who has to sell quotas of space on time and will be delighted to know that you can be called at short notice. You will also get some really great deals – sometimes as much as 80 per cent off rate card!

If you really want to be clever, find out the copy date (the last date for artwork to be submitted) and call the paper/magazine just beforehand. They will sometimes let space go at silly prices, just so as to avoid blank pages. Have your bromides ready and negotiate a bargain. You will find that 5.30 p.m. is a great time to pick up deals on daily papers. The deadline is running out for the sales department and you can say 'yes' or 'no' immediately without the need for a committee meeting. In return you will get the best rates. Occasionally, you might even get a better deal than would be offered to a media buyer, because the advertisement sales people don't always want the industry to know how far they are prepared to discount. The most important piece of advice I can give you is to buy late and buy cheap; it's the only way to make money. Reuben Ash of

Drive Innovations (marketers of new, innovative mail order products) has adopted a very simple system of obtaining good discounts and he is entirely self-taught! He simply sends his bromides to the relevant papers and asks them to ring him when they have space at an 80 per cent discount – and only when! They might not appear happy at the proposition, but almost invariably call back with an offer. Not bad for a beginner who confesses: 'When I first started, I was having trouble negotiating a 10 per cent discount!'

In return, be professional and always pay your bills on time. To begin with, pay up front if requested. When you have a track record, ask to be invoiced and pay on 30 days. If you have a complaint about your ad, put it in writing immediately, negotiate a discount if appropriate, but don't jeopardise your relationship with the media/paper. These people are your lifeline.

Never forget – most media have their rivals; if done skilfully, you can play one against the other to secure the best rate. Also remember that you can play upon a paper's weakness. For example, take a publication that specialises in lots of small ads such as *Exchange & Mart*. They rarely sell full-page ads, but would no doubt like to and would therefore probably be prepared to deal on a page rate. Similarly, any newly-established media will have to set the ball rolling by offering special deals.

A final word of caution

It should be noted that you won't always be able to insist upon a discount and it is important to know when not to push your request, if only to remain on good terms with the advertising sales executive. Sometimes a paper/magazine will find that its space is selling well; it may be the time of year, general economic optimism or just a good sales team. Whichever, they will seize upon the opportunity to charge full rate card and just refuse to deal. Accept that this is the case and move on.

Similarly, if they notice that your product is doing well and appearing all over the place, they will sometimes try to charge more, simply because they know you can afford it. In these cases, remember the golden rule:

Never be pressurised to pay over the odds for any advertisement, however much you want it. You simply won't make money.

9

THE
FULFILMENT
PROCESS

I F YOU HAVE followed this book from the beginning, you have by now found a suitable product, booked those advertisements and are eagerly awaiting the results. But, hold on, you are still only half-way towards running a successful mail order business. The next and equally important phase is the fulfilment – the process whereby you dispatch the product to the customer. Fulfilment is not difficult, but it does require attention to detail, speed, accuracy and, above all, having a system. For this reason specialist companies have sprung up all over the UK, just for the purpose of handling these aspects of the mail order operation. For some businesses they are an efficient and economical alternative to doing it yourself (see page 156).

If you are still a small concern, you will probably want to control the fulfilment yourself. This is quite feasible and is, in essence, just a scaled-down version of the professional fulfilment house system, the key to which is organisation.

HOW TO DISPATCH CUSTOMER ORDERS

The fulfilment process follows a fairly logical set of steps.

1. Receiving, opening and sorting all orders

Your goal here is twofold.

- to sort the mail into product groups, so that if you are selling more than one item you can identify who has ordered what;
- within these groups, to sort by media code, so that you can prepare the daily report sheets as explained below in step 2.

The most efficient way to do this is to reserve a large table space specifically for handling mail. Don't put your mail anywhere else. Loose envelopes and flimsy coupons can easily get lost among the other paraphernalia of fulfilment. Before you even open the letters, divide the mail into coded and non-coded envelopes. A coded envelope means that the person has responded to a non-couponed ad and should be put in one pile; an uncoded envelope suggests that the contents are either a coupon or a piece of general correspondence and should be put into a second pile.

Take great care when opening the envelopes – cheques are easily torn in half, especially by letter openers, and will not be accepted by the bank even if sellotaped back together. You will invariably find that some envelopes contain orders but no cheques or they do have cheques but no indication of an address! In the former instance, send a pre-printed note requesting the cheque with the customer's name and address. In the latter, return the cheque to the bank branch it was issued from with a request to forward it to the customer.

Sort the orders by product and, within that, by media code; it is a good idea to use small cardboard boxes to keep the bits of paper separate and organised. Be especially careful that you sort non-couponed orders into the correct 'media boxes'; because, if you remember, the code is no longer obvious once you have thrown away the envelope. For this reason also it is normal to prepare the results sheets next.

2. Compiling a daily report sheet

This is where accuracy becomes of paramount importance. Your subsequent decision to spend hard-earned money on further advertising stems from the information on these sheets. It may seem time-consuming, but the layout shown on page 150 is well worth following.

Keep a separate sheet for each product, date it and always keep it on file for future reference. Notice the distinction made between cash and credit card orders. It is important to monitor credit card sales as a percentage of total orders, especially since they are more costly to process. Sometimes your cash and credit card values will not be straight multiples of the numbers ordered – this is because people occasionally make mistakes when writing out the cheque and underpay by a few pence. If the amount concerned is under 50p, I would ignore it and process the order – correcting the mistake would cost more in stamps alone! You will also find that people send in orders with no code at all; these have to be listed on a 'miscellaneous' sheet.

3. Transferring customer details on to address labels

Here you have a decision to make. You can either adopt a manual system or invest in a computer. Basically, there are two jobs to be done:

- recording the customer's name, address, postcode etc. for future reference;

Daily Report Sheet

Name of product : Quilted Waistcoat

Unit price : £19.95

Date : 8.4.94

Code	No of orders			£ Value of orders		
	Cash	c/c	Total	Cash	c/c	Total
TI 23 11 93	1	—	1	19.95	—	19.95
Te 11 01 94	2	1	3	39.90	19.95	59.85
Su 22 02 94	1	—	1	19.95	—	19.95
Gu 05 03 94	3	1	4	59.85	19.95	79.80
Ih 02 04 94	10	3	13	199.50	59.85	259.35
Obs 27 03 94	15	8	23	299.25	159.60	458.85
mS 08 04 94	18	7	25	359.10	139.65	498.75
lonS 03 04 94	14	5	19	279.30	99.50	378.80
No of returns: 3						
Totals	64	25	89	1276.80	498.50	1775.30

- preparing an address label for dispatch of goods.

Operating a manual system is obviously cheaper as you don't have the initial outlay for equipment. It is also no more time-consuming than using a computer. The time spent addressing labels by hand is balanced by the fact that you store names and addresses via the original coupon/letter rather than having to type them into the computer. However, technology does offer some advantages. Once the customer information is typed on to the screen (now you'll be pleased that you asked the customer to write in block capitals!), it can be organised alphabetically by surname and in groups by product; even to the point where you can identify who has bought more than once, what they bought and when, all of which is good marketing information. You will also be able to print off the address labels, a great time saver, especially if you ever wish to send out a second mailing to the same people.

It should be stressed that there is no absolute need for a computer when you start out, but if you can spare a few hundred pounds, shop around for a basic computer, printer (with label facility) and word-processing software package. The high street electrical stores all stock a variety of makes, some of them very good value for money and not at all difficult to master.

4. Packaging and sending off the product

Again, you need to dedicate a specific corner of the room to this part of the operation. The best approach is to keep the product(s) stored separately around the perimeter of the allocated space, and have a central table/bench on which you package up the orders, one product at a time. To avoid confusion, put the product back in its allocated space once packaged, ready to go to the post office. Your 'assembly line' will vary, depending upon the nature of the product. Basically, you should work from left to right, starting with the product and then adding any other promotional/sales material (see Chapters 10 and 12). It is entirely optional as to whether or not you enclose a receipt with the order; this applies to credit card orders as well as cheques. It may be a good idea not to because of the administration involved, but you should always issue a receipt upon request.

Your choice of packaging will depend upon the size, shape and fragility of the item, but here are some general tips.

- It is always better to 'over' pack than to skimp on materials. Your product costs more than the padding and you will have to bear the cost of replacing a damaged item. Good packaging also gives a good impression to the customer.
- Padded envelopes are wonderful, but expensive. It is much cheaper to buy bubble bags (the plastic sheeting with 'built-in' air pockets that cushion against knocks) separately and then put them into the envelopes. Make sure you buy the right dimensions so that they fit into each other.
- Never leave too much space between the product and the packaging. If the goods are rattling around, they are more likely to be damaged in transit.
- Always go for light and strong packaging materials. Anything dense and heavy could push you into the next postal bracket. If in doubt, ask the advice of your post office.
- Buy materials in bulk wherever possible – it saves money. Go to wholesale merchants rather than high street retail outlets, or better still, direct to the manufacturer; good old *Yellow Pages* comes in handy here. Look under 'Packaging materials'.

Once you have packaged the product and additional material, seal the envelope/box and affix the address label. Your final task is to work out the postage. A pair of PO-approved scales would be very useful, with the advantage of the postal rates being printed alongside the weight bands. If your volume of post is significant, you could opt for a franking machine – this automatically prints the postage on the envelope. But bear in mind that although it may save you time, the machine costs money to buy and is only really efficient when handling items of the same postal value.

You must also be prepared for a daily trek to the PO; they will only come and collect when you have over 1,000 items in one posting – and you would be very foolish to stockpile orders until that figure was reached (more about timing at the end of this chapter).

Unfortunately, there are no discounts on postal rates either, unless you handle more than 4,000 items per posting. At this point you can use a system called Mailsort, whereby you sort and bag the mail by postcode, thus qualifying for a discount of between 13 and 25 per cent on postage rates, depending upon how many days you are prepared to allow for delivery. To set up an account you should contact Royal Mail Streamline (details at the back of this book).

Be extra careful if you are sending out orders of more than one product; you must allow for the increase in both postage and packing. Also, remember that second-class post is only defined as such up to a weight of 750 grammes, above which the package has to go first class! Under normal circumstances, I would always opt for the postal saving and send out by second-class mail.

5. Banking moneys received

The majority of people send cheques, then credit card orders and a small number send cash or postal orders. Obviously, you will want to bank your money as quickly as possible for cash flow reasons etc., but MOPS recommends that cheques only be banked if you have the product ready to send out and do so within the 21 or 28 days promised. You can, of course, bank the cheque after you have sent out the goods, but in doing so you will occasionally have to suffer a bounced cheque after the product has been dispatched!

Credit card orders can only be processed after you have dispatched the goods. This ruling will appear in any credit card agreement you sign. Having said that, there is also a ruling which says they have to be presented to the bank within five days of dispatching goods in order to remain valid (this varies slightly depending upon the handling house). So you really have to be ready and waiting when those orders come in.

Cheques
The best way to bank cheques is to sort them first according to product and then list the cheque totals for each product on separate paying-in slips. These figures should, of course, tally with your daily analysis sheet totals. It goes without saying that you should aim to bank money on a daily basis.

Credit cards
Credit card orders are processed by transferring the details given in the advertisement on to the credit card summary sheets, again on a per product basis. The sheet will vary in appearance depending upon which bank you go through, but the procedure is the same – you simply pay it in at the bank with your other money.

Beware that people sometimes inadvertently misquote their card numbers; the most common problem is omission of a digit. Visa and Access cards always have either 4 digits + (3×4) digits, i.e. 16 in total or 4 digits + (3×3) digits, i.e. 13 in total.

Cash
Cash is occasionally sent. There are still quite a few people who do not have bank accounts! This is good for you, because cash gets credited immediately to the bank account, but fiddly in every other respect and less easy to trace should there be a query with the order. Never offer the option of cash payments in your advertisements.

Postal orders
People without bank accounts also send postal orders. These are better than cash because the sender has a receipt as proof. Simply bank them along with everything else, marking them on your paying-in slips as postal orders.

6. Handling returns

We shall be looking at the philosophy and mechanics of refunding in more detail in Chapter 10. Suffice to say here that refund requests will usually be accompanied by the returned product, which must not be put back in with the main body of stock. These items are not normally suitable for resale – so don't offer them again. Your best bet is to either give them away to a good cause (we give our returned books to a local hospital each quarter) or destroy them. Lastly, don't forget to enter the number of returns on the daily analysis sheet.

7. Holding stock and monitoring stock levels

If your stock is being delivered to you, always check that the quantities and condition are as agreed before you sign the delivery note.

Depending upon the size, shape, quantity and nature of your product, you will need either a room set aside for storage, or to be able to put the items directly into the packaging and dispatch area. If you do need a separate storage area, make sure that it is dry and secure. You will also need to increase your insurance premiums.

In the early stages, it is better to keep stock levels low so as not to tie up too much capital. But legally you must have sufficient stock to cover expected response. You must also be prepared for a sudden rush of orders and be sure that you can access extra stock at short notice. The publishing business is quite flexible in this respect – we only ever start with a print-run of 1,000 books, but can reprint up to 10,000 books within a few days should there be a sudden demand. Even with our track record of success, we would never be so presumptuous as to overstock before we had gauged the market reaction.

Most important, adjust your stock level figure daily, after the analysis sheets have been written up and think ahead as to how much or how little stock you are likely to need. If you are dependent upon a supplier, build extra time into your schedules. Otherwise you could be left with a lot of customers and nothing to send them.

DO YOU NEED A FULFILMENT HOUSE?

As you will now realise, it is perfectly feasible to handle your own fulfilment and there are several major advantages to doing so.

- **Control over procedure**   You can make sure that orders are going out well packaged, on time and with the correct inserts. You will also be better informed when dealing with customer complaints relating to late delivery etc.
- **Control over money**   This is an important one. You are hardly likely to cheat yourself and there is no better person to do the banking. The vast majority of fulfilment houses are 100 per cent honest, but it has been known for a few of them to divert funds and, in one or two spectacular cases, to misappropriate thousands of pounds! It is simple common sense for you to impose a system of checks on anyone who handles your money – ask for weekly and possibly even daily bank statements, so that you can make sure that the amounts banked tally with the analysis sheets and paying-in slips. It goes without saying that all customer cheques should be made out to your trading name and banked into your bank account. Do not have money diverted through the fulfilment house bank account (although some companies do). If they insist, find another fulfilment house. However much you trust/like someone, remember that money is a huge temptation. If in doubt, bank it yourself!

- **Control over stock**   Obviously, no one will care about your stock as much as you do. If it is being held on someone else's premises insist upon regular stocktaking. Make sure that they also have adequate insurance and get confirmation of that in writing.

Advantages of fulfilment houses

Having said all the above, fulfilment houses do come into their own when a mail order operation gets too large to handle alone. Their particular strengths are as follows.

Dedicated resources

Fulfilment houses exist specifically to 'fulfil' and have these dedicated resources.

- Different stages of the operation are allocated separate rooms.
- Storage is usually plentiful.
- Specialist and often expensive equipment is at your disposal, e.g. forklift trucks for moving large volumes of stock.
- Personnel and time. Fulfilment houses can devote whole teams of people and the whole day to opening the mail and dispatching the goods. You are far less flexible – fulfilment is only one of your daily tasks and all it takes is a slightly larger post than expected and you might start to fall behind. A fulfilment house has the resources to react quickly to change and, for instance, to accommodate another insert/customer promotion. On your own you might not be able to do this and you could miss an opportunity.

Computer equipment

Fulfilment houses invariably operate sophisticated computer systems with huge memory capacity. Often millions of names and addresses are stored on one machine. Obviously, you don't need this, but you can benefit from some of the specialist database programs; the 'quick address' program, for instance, which can scan any postcode in the country and tell you in seconds whether or not the accompanying address is correct – a godsend for checking people's handwriting! Computers also make light work of large address label runs and mailshots, things that would take hours to do by hand. Most of all, however, you will need the use of a computer for renting out your customer names, something that can make as much money as the mail order operation itself (see Chapter 12).

Economies of scale
Because fulfilment houses deal with several clients at a time, they can command big discounts on envelopes, packaging, printing etc., some of which will be passed on to you.

HOW TO FIND A FULFILMENT HOUSE

You might decide that you want to use a fulfilment house right from the start. They vary greatly in size and cost, but should all be able to perform roughly the same functions. Your best bet is to seek recommendations from other mail order companies and look for a fulfilment house that specialises in your product area, i.e. clothes, gifts, books etc. Specialist houses will be more familiar with the requirements for processing that particular item and will probably be more efficient. You should also contact the Direct Mail Services Standards Board (address at the back of this book), who produce a booklet, free of charge, listing their fulfilment members, all of whom have to provide three years' accounts and two guarantees before being accepted as members. You don't necessarily have to choose a 'big house' in the business. You might wish to start with a smaller operation that has some 'dead time' and could profit by slotting you in.

THE COST OF FULFILMENT

The best way to understand the cost of fulfilment is to break down the process of fulfilment into various components and look at what a fulfilment house might charge compared to your own costs. Separating out the charges will also help you to negotiate more effectively when discussing fees and to pinpoint areas that are costing too much. Consider the table below:

Function	Cost per 1,000 items	
	Fulfilment House	In-house
1. Opening and sorting the mail and compiling daily analysis sheets	£140	Cost of your time
2. Putting customer names and address on to computer	£80	Cost of your time plus purchase of computer
3. Running off labels (incl. cost of labels)	£8–£10	Cost of time plus £5 per 1,000 approx for labels
4. Packaging the item	£65, depending on the number of items packaged	Cost of your time
5. Envelope/ package cost	*Depends on item	Slightly higher than fulfilment house because not the same bulk rates

	Cost per 1,000 items	
Function	Fulfilment House	In-house
6. Sticking on address labels and stamps	£15	Cost of your time
7. Stamp cost	At cost	At cost
8. Banking money	£10 (credit cards cost more – £20 per 1,000)	Cost of your time
9. Storage charges	£100 per month per 100 sq ft	Cost of having a room in your house effectively out of action for any other purpose
10. Handling refunds	20p each plus cost of env/postage/bank charge for cheque/ compliments slip	Cost of your time and costs as for fulfilment house

*If you were using a C4 envelope (approx 5p each) and a bubble bag to go inside (approx 3p), the cost would be approx 8p in total per item

These fulfilment house costs are average for 1993/4, for volumes of not less than 2,000 items per week. You must expect to pay more if you use a fulfilment house in the early stages of your business when volumes are lower. Do shop around, as costs can vary considerably and you could end up paying a lot more than outlined above.

Bear in mind that you should pay postage immediately or in advance, since the stamps have already been paid for by the time the order goes out. Everything else will probably be invoiced weekly. Given that mail order is a positive cash flow business, and to maintain goodwill, I would pay these invoices by return of post.

Obviously, the cost of fulfilment will fluctuate according to postage rates, packaging materials, salary increases etc., so you must always keep an eye on it. Make sure that any increases are compensated for by cost-cutting elsewhere or an equivalent price increase in your product. Otherwise you will find that the fulfilment starts eating into your gross profit margin. Never be complacent – keep checking both your direct and indirect product costs (refer back to Chapter 4 if necessary).

THE IMPORTANCE OF BEING PROMPT!

We have already looked at the organisation involved in receiving and dispatching orders, but it is also important to consider timing. Any fulfilment house worth its salt will already practise the principle laid out below. But you should still note the following.

In your advertisement you have told the customer to expect delivery within 21 days (I always think that 28 days is too long to expect someone to wait). They will see this as a promise and it is one you must keep at all costs. If you fall at this early fence you will have lost your customer's trust before you've really started. Bear in mind that the customer starts counting from the day they cut out the coupon. They may take another day or two to put it in the post – second class usually – so by the time it reaches you, 6 or 7 of your 21 days have already elapsed. Don't even think of saying 'That's not fair'. That is mail order, and you must be ready and waiting at your end. But there are several things you can do to stay one step ahead.

Open all the mail the day you receive it

This may sound obvious and will not present a problem in the early stages of your business when the mail is relatively light. None the less, use the system outlined earlier for opening and sorting the mail. It will stand you in good stead when your business picks up.

When we started marketing the *Government Auction Handbook* we suddenly found ourselves with 5,000 orders a day and only three people to open the mail. If it takes a minute to open and sort an order, 5,000 orders will take about 83 hours, i.e. about 27 hours per person – in an 8-hour working day! Needless to say, we were taken by surprise and immediately had to draft in more people to avoid unacceptable delays. And remember, if you don't get the first day's post opened and dispatched within 24 hours, the second batch of post pours through the door and creates an insurmountable backlog. It all causes unnecessary aggravation – both for you and the customer, who quite frankly doesn't care how many other orders there are. That's your problem. So be prepared and open all mail the day you receive it.

Send out the product the same day

In the best of all worlds you receive the order in the morning and have the product in the afternoon post. If you can do this, the customer will probably have his item within 10 days of seeing the advertisement, not 21. That is impressive. It says more about you than any self-congratulatory comment in the advertising copy ever will. Past Times aims to deliver within only seven days of receipt of order, a marvellous achievement for a company of this size. And people do appreciate it – my company has had letters from customers who wrote simply to thank us for being so prompt (more about that later). It means that you can afford to send out the product by second-class post, which will save you a small fortune over the year. It also means that you have kept your first promise to the customer, who now trusts you and will be far more likely to order again. The only qualification I must make to this advice is that some cheques will inevitably bounce after you have dispatched the goods. Unfortunately, you just have to build this into your costs, and the small numbers involved do not justify delaying dispatch of all items until the cheques have cleared.

10

CUSTOMER

SERVICE

WHY CUSTOMER SERVICE WILL MAKE OR BREAK YOU

CUSTOMER SERVICE is viewed by many as a necessary chore. They couldn't be more wrong! It presents a marvellous opportunity and is absolutely vital to the ongoing success of any business. An unhappy customer will not only think twice about buying again, but will also tell all their friends – and bad news travels fast. On the other hand a happy customer may well stay loyal to you for years.

Customer service really does have the capacity to make or break your business. How can we forget that ill-judged comment which sent the share price of Gerald Ratner's company plummeting? Ratner's customers simply weren't going to let him get away with what they saw as an insult and voted by staying out of Ratner's shops. No customers, no business.

That was a high street retail situation. In the mail order world customer service is even more important. You have no shop front, just an advertisement. Your customer cannot see or speak to you. They are at quite a disadvantage and it is therefore a great act of trust on their part to send money, and for your part you must be prompt, thorough, ethical and courteous in all dealings. Michelle Kershaw, Customer Director of Lakeland Plastics, says quite simply that customer service 'is why we are where we are today. We look at the customer's problem and come up with the answer.'

What is customer service?

The British have a reputation for being sloppy when it comes to looking after their customers and part of the problem is that we fail to understand the true meaning of customer service. We have long since come to associate it with a negative feeling and to assume that:

> 'Customer service = customer complaints = us against them and unfortunately we have to pretend that the customer is always right.'

This simply isn't so. Customer service is an ongoing procedure. It starts from the moment you receive someone's order and covers all aspects of dispatch, further offers, special requests and, yes, also the complaints. Far from being on opposite sides of the fence, customer service is about cultivating a relationship that will last and, incidentally, one which will make you real money from repeat orders. How many times have you sat in a restaurant after a bad meal, smiled weakly when asked if everything was all right, but left vowing never to go there again? The restaurant will never improve its standards because they think that you left satisfied and will be mightily confused when they notice that no one ever comes back!

Customer satisfaction is your lifeblood. If you handle your customers properly from the beginning you will not only minimise complaints and refund requests, but will also learn how to get some of your most convincing publicity free of charge – in the form of customer testimonials. Far from being a chore, customer service is a terrific way to understand your customers, and thus to promote and expand the business. Best of all, it costs you very little. You will really stand out in your 'market place', especially when so many others fail to understand the basic principles. Look at almost any successful company you care to mention: Marks & Spencer, Virgin, John Lewis Partnership etc. They all know how to look after their customers and the customers respond by coming back. So always remember:

- **customer service is fundamental to your success;**
- **customer service presents opportunities not problems.**

In the mail order business these opportunities start the moment you receive your first order and fall into the following categories.

DISPATCHING ORDERS

It makes great marketing sense to send a thank you note with the order. It is your first chance to start building a relationship with the customer and to develop the 'feel good' factor. Let them know that you value their order and pave the way for future offers. For example:

From: Smithco Ltd, 37 Jones Street, London SW2 1AP

Dear Customer,
Thank you for your order and here, enclosed, is the
_____ that you requested. We hope you will enjoy
this _____ and that we can continue to serve you
with further items in the future.

*In addition, we hope to be able, from time to time, to
bring you interesting offers from other reputable
companies. Should you prefer not to receive such offers,
please write to us here at the above address.

In the mean time, thank you once again for your order
and we look forward to sending you useful and
interesting offers in the future.

With compliments

This will all fit on to a normal-sized compliments slip and can be popped in with each order. In addition, the paragraph marked with an asterisk* is useful if you haven't been able to fit a data protection clause into the original advertisement (see Chapter 6) but do want the option of renting your customer names.

What do I do if there is a time delay?

The other major point to consider when dispatching orders is that you must have a backup system ready in case of delay. Obviously, not everyone will have their product ready to send out the same day. It may be that you are producing goods to order, such as clothes, personalised stationery, pet portraits or that you have suddenly run out of stock and need time to get more in. Whatever the reason, communicate this to your customer. If you don't, they will think you are neglecting them, or worse still, have run off with the money! Try to remember that they cannot see what is going on. All you need do is send an interim note, explain the situation clearly, give an estimate of when the item will be ready for dispatch and if the delay has been an unexpected one, giving the customer the option to cancel their order. See the example overleaf.

You think that the last offer is asking for trouble? Not so. You will find that very few people cancel their order. After all, they probably do still want the item, will be greatly reassured that you have taken the trouble to keep them informed and feel that having come this far they should continue. Far from damaging your reputation, the offer to cancel will add greatly to your credibility.

Dear Sir/Madam,

Thank you for your valued order. I am sorry to have to write and tell you that there has been a delay with delivery of the item, and it will be another ten days before we can dispatch the order to you. I understand your disappointment and can assure you that we are doing all we can to get your order to you as quickly as possible. If, however, you do wish to cancel because of the delay, please either call or write to us and we shall return your payment immediately. Once again, please accept our apologies for the inconvenience and may we thank you for your patience.

Yours sincerely,

Taking the opportunity to sell again . . .

There is one last point to note here. Some companies make a lot of money by selling again to the customer before the first order has arrived. They strike whilst the iron is hot! The customer is keen and eagerly anticipating their purchase. The company writes to them, confirming that delivery will indeed be within, say, 21 days and use the same correspondence to make another offer. For example, an American company which sells giant vegetable seeds, operates a smart system. When the initial order has been received, they send out an interim letter to the customer while the item is being processed. See opposite.

They estimate that this simple device results in a 12–15 per cent response (most people would be happy with a 3–5 per cent result with this type of marketing) and generates double the profit margin of the initial offer! Not bad for a simple sales letter. This is in part due to the fact that they are targeting

Dear Sir/Madam,

Thank you for your recent order for our Miracle Bush Tomatoes.

As you may know, each section of the country has a different growing season. We will send you your Miracle Bush Tomatoes at the exact right time for planting where you live. This assures that your plants will grow well, and produce the largest possible yield.

In the mean time, take a look at the special plant offers from MBT nursery sales enclosed. Each is an exciting giant variety that is easy and fun to grow. And each produces just about the most amazing fruit of its kind.

Of course you can always buy with confidence from MBT nursery sales. Every plant variety we offer is guaranteed to grow and thrive in your garden, or let us know any time – even next fall after the growing season is over – and we'll promptly refund your entire purchase price.

And – if your order totals $7.00 or more, we'll also send you a Surprise Nursery Pack with a retail value of $5.00 or more – absolutely free!

So look through the colorful offers and place your order right now.

Happy gardening!

MBT Nursery Sales.

(Reproduced with the kind permission of Mr Wesley Wood and MBT Nursery Sales, New York, USA)

known seed purchasers who are therefore more likely to buy, and partly because it is only costing them the price of the letter and a stamp to try and sell a second time round – but it all leads to extra profit! So if you have a natural 'follow-on' product, that could be the time to sell it. Remember, you should always look for an opportunity.

HANDLING GENERAL QUERIES

General queries can lead to all sorts of openings and often directly to an order. So don't be tempted to ignore them. Most important, you should aim to build up a reputation for the following.

Promptness

At the risk of labouring the point, do try to open and answer the query on the same day. It achieves two things. First, it improves your own productivity and second, if people have to wait weeks for a reply they will invariably lose interest and you have then lost potential business.

Efficiency

Keep on file copies of all your correspondence with enquirers, both your response and the enquirers' original letter (alphabetically by surname makes easy reference). If you have a telephone number, call as well – it's your chance to present the voice of the company and also speed things up; take that opportunity also to ask the person what they do and don't want from your mail order service. Learn to listen, because customer comments will tell you how you should be shaping the business – which products you should be offering and what makes people respond to your ads.

It is also worth mentioning that you should make sure that your own telephone number is clearly listed in directory enquiries. Quite apart from the obvious question of convenience, there is nothing more frustrating or worrying for a customer than to discover that you are not on the telephone. It is very reassuring for them to be able to hear the voice of the company, and the direct contact means that they are less likely to take their problem elsewhere, i.e. to the newspapers which carried the advertisement – something which will damage your reputation and is to be avoided at all costs. John Beale of Past Times regards the telephone as a vital tool in customer service, allowing him to 'solve problems instantly.'

Information

Be informed, both about the customer and the product. Have all the facts at your fingertips and make sure you are in control when being asked about your products, especially on the telephone. It simply doesn't look good if you don't know the stock level/price/size etc. of an item. This becomes especially important when the business grows and you have employees – involve everyone in knowing their product range.

Similarly, use your customer files, so that if someone rings a second time, you are familiar with their background and previous enquiry. I recently called a London newspaper with which I had placed an advert, worried because I wanted to ensure that an important amendment had been made. The company employs over 200 people, but the telephonist was able to refer to the card system and tell me within seconds that the amendment was in hand. She even knew to whom I had spoken earlier that day. I was instantly reassured and very impressed – and it really isn't very difficult to achieve such service.

Preparedness

Anticipate your customer queries. Save time by having standard response slips for the most common requests – all you need do is sign them. In the mail order business you will most frequently be asked for information on these issues.

- **The product** Compose a standard reply on a single A5 or A4 sheet of paper. Don't make it too complicated – you can talk yourself out of a sale! And don't think that it has to be on expensive paper; black type (not handwritten) on simple 80 gm weight paper is fine. After all, it's the information that the customer wants, nothing else at this stage. They can actually be put off if they think you are squandering money on expensive presentation. Far from impressing and encouraging them, it can have quite the opposite effect!

- **How to order**   Sometimes people hear about the item from a friend or buy the paper but accidentally throw it away. Have ready a stack of photocopied ads and a response mechanism.
- **The company's other products**   Again, a straight-forward typed sheet will suffice until such time as you might expand and develop a catalogue.
- **Trade terms**   This is important. Never forget that your customers will be both private individuals and other business people. Dealing with the latter also comes under 'customer service' and can lead to valuable large orders. Decide first though if you want to sell in bulk for subsequent resale; you may have made a feature of the fact that your product is unique and only available from one source, and you wouldn't want to destroy this USP.

If you are happy to sell to the trade, decide in advance what discount you can afford to give (maybe on a sliding scale according to the size of the order) and be firm. Bulk sales are a great way to shift stock and make a quick profit, but only if you have sold at the right price and that includes taking into account all product costs, direct and indirect, right down to the cost of delivery to the customer (refer back to Chapter 4 if necessary).

Answer every query

Never be tempted to ignore general correspondence, just because it isn't accompanied by an instant cheque. These queries are building blocks which can lead to future orders. It is also a golden opportunity to spread the word about your other products/developments/special offers etc. Mail order companies spend a lot of time and money trying to identify which people to write to, i.e. who would be most likely to buy the product. Here they have identified themselves and come to you asking for information – what more could you want? There is very little selling to do, so don't neglect it; give them comprehensive and well-presented responses – promptly!

HANDLING SPECIFIC COMPLAINTS

This is the area most commonly associated with the term 'customer service' and the one which has given it a negative image. It is certainly a delicate issue but one which, handled sensitively, will do wonders for your image and will not necessarily lose you a customer. Always remember:

Everyone makes mistakes, it is how you handle them that counts.

Whatever you do, don't ignore the complaint and hope that the customer will go away. They will not. The psychology of mail order is such that because the customer cannot see you, there is an increased sense of anxiety when something goes wrong and a tendency to overreact in an effort to attract attention to their plight. You can diffuse this by being seen to tackle the problem quickly and by seeking a mutually acceptable answer rather than by counter-attacking. Avoid confrontation. Begin by apologising for any inconvenience and then offer possible solutions.

All of this can be done either by letter or by phone. The latter is more immediate and shows that you are going to some trouble to put the matter right, but it is also expensive. Most of the time a letter is enough. If you make this effort it is also less likely that the customer will take the matter further. At all costs avoid a situation where the customer goes to MOPS or the ASA etc., because you will then have several people breathing down your neck and an official black mark on your score card.

The most common complaints

First, however, you have to be aware of the different types of complaints you might be faced with and how you can avoid them in the first place.

First impressions

The very nature of mail order, i.e. that the customer generally pays for the item before they actually see it, means that you will find that a proportion of complaints relate to the appearance of the item, that it:

- doesn't match the description of the advertisement;
- isn't value for money;
- is the wrong shape/colour/size, etc.;
- 'it just isn't what I expected!'

None of these complaints would arise from a shop-bought item which is seen and handled before purchase. But in mail order you find that the reality of the product sometimes fails to meet the customer's expectations. This is because no two people will interpret a piece of advertising copy in quite the same way. They will read into it pretty much what they want to see (especially if they have to persuade themselves that it is a worthwhile purchase) and in the process will probably distort the true picture of the item. Add to that the anticipation and excitement of receiving a package through the post, and you can understand why the item itself can be quite an anti-climax.

Sometimes there are quite straightforward ways of avoiding this situation. For example, the Past Times catalogues always illustrate jewellery to its actual size. Occasionally the problem is slightly more complex, as we discovered when selling our giant tomato seeds. Although the advertisement stated quite clearly that we were selling seeds and repeated the information in the coupon, a number of people queried the fact that they had received 'just a packet of seeds' and not tomato plants or, in some cases, the tomatoes themselves! Part of the explanation was that we had so successfully painted the picture of huge, luscious fruits that many customers had chosen to ignore the fact that they would have to grow the tomatoes from seed.

We solved this problem with a very simple device. When we enclosed the 'thank you' slip with the seeds we incorporated a few extra sentences at the beginning which reiterated the benefits of the product; that the size, taste, yield, appearance etc. was exceptional. This meant that as the customer opened the package they were reminded of all the reasons that made them purchase the product in the first place and they served to reaffirm their faith in the item at this crucial moment. I say 'crucial' because it is at this point that most people will make that snap decision to either keep or return the item and this simple measure can significantly reduce your returns. So, never forget, use your 'thank you' slip to restate the benefits of the product as given in the original advertisement.

That the item is technically substandard
This could mean that the product has arrived broken, damaged or with missing components. You can avoid the majority of these complaints by checking each item as it is packaged. Build this into the fulfilment process and devise a checklist of the main things the packager should look for. Once the item is in the post it is effectively beyond your control and accidents do happen; we have had mail lost, defaced and even stolen. For this very reason most mail order companies do not deal with especially fragile or valuable items. If you must do so, it is worth considering a special form of delivery (remember to build this into your product cost) and, of course, insurance will be essential.

That the product arrived late or, worse still, has not yet arrived
The importance of prompt dispatch has already been stressed. Postal delays are not unknown, so you need to give yourself the maximum advantage by posting as quickly as possible. To be honest, if an item arrives late and the customer complains, you

can only apologise and give an adequate explanation (if there is one). If the item has not yet arrived when the customer rings, I would also give them the chance to cancel. It is usually far more effective to meet a complaint with sympathy and agreement than with denial, and you will find that very few people take up the offer; you have apologised and reassured them, and that is really what they wanted to hear. Mail order moguls often have to be amateur psychologists as well!

Miscellaneous reasons

Such a reason could be that the item is no longer wanted or that the person can no longer afford it etc. These may sound like weak excuses, but they do occur. Sometimes the reason is genuine, i.e. someone has lost their job. Sometimes it relates to the point made earlier – that the reality has failed to meet the customer's expectations and they feel too embarrassed to say so. Whatever the reason, be it appearance, late delivery, faulty goods, and however unfair you think it is to your business, the customer has a right to satisfaction. Obviously there is very little you can do in these cases to anticipate the problem. The next best remedy is to offer the customer the chance to return the item and claim a refund. (It always helps to enclose an s.a.e. of the right size for return of goods, so that the customer does not have to bear the postage costs.) This is a most important part of customer service and one we shall look at next.

REFUNDS AND RETURNS

You need only remember one thing:

always offer a full, no-questions-asked, money-back guarantee on all items sold through your business.

The benefits in terms of your credibility are enormous. Not only will people feel more comfortable about purchasing in the first place, but they are actually less likely to request a refund, simply because you were seen to play fair and gave them a feeling of security. You will have noticed that all the advertisements shown in Chapter 7 carried the money-back guarantee. Most successful mail order companies pay great attention to this aspect of their operation. Lakeland Plastics offer a lifetime guarantee on their products – something you don't often get from a shop-bought item (see page 214).

You may wonder how many people tamper with/use the product and then return it. The answer, actually, is far fewer than you might imagine. Of course it does happen and it is very frustrating for us when a customer returns a book with a broken spine and coffee stains (as they have done). But thankfully only one or two in every thousand do so. And yes, we do still give them a full refund, simply because we cannot prove that they have read the book, and it isn't worth the effort to try and do so. Unfair? Yes, of course it is unfair. But thankfully it is only a minor and occasional irritation. Most people are scrupulously honest and a pleasure to deal with.

Conditions of refund

You should make very few conditions, for the reasons outlined above, but do ask for the following.

Customers must return the item in order to qualify for a refund

Obviously you need some proof that the person did actually purchase the item in the first place, otherwise you are inviting people to take advantage. Also, if the item is faulty you will want to examine it and make appropriate changes to your production methods.

Your total returns on any one product will usually be about 5 per cent of sales, but this can vary from product to product.

Clothing, for example, is often much higher because of problems with size and fit. The important thing to look out for is an abnormally high level of returns. It suggests that the product is fundamentally flawed and you should try to find out why without delay. You should make a point of checking the returns figure every day.

Customers must request the refund within 30 days of purchase

Thirty days is a reasonable time for the customer to decide whether or not the product is suitable. This is the length of time we state in all our advertisements. It also helps us gauge the success/failure of a product if we know that most of the returns will be made within the 30-day period. In practice however, we issue a refund regardless of when the item comes back to us, as a simple gesture of courtesy and good business practice. It is seldom abused.

Mechanics of refunding

This is very straightforward. Always refund by cheque if possible (some people may request a credit card refund if they paid that way) – it allows you to keep a more accurate record of the amounts involved. When your business has expanded, there will inevitably be more refunds to handle and it will become very time-consuming (not to mention dull). You can, however, get rubber stamps made up with the different product amounts, which means that all you have to do is sign the cheques and fill in the customer's name. In the meantime, make a point of refunding on the day you get the request. Send the customer the cheque and a short accompanying note (see opposite page).

If the circumstances are exceptional and you think it appropriate to make 'extra' amends, enclose a small gift as well; we sometimes send another book. But do be sensitive and make the gift appropriate. We publish a helpful book called *Write Your Own Will*, but you can imagine how that could be misconstrued by the recipient! Needless to say, it is not on our gift list.

Dear

Thank you for your letter, and I'm very sorry to hear you have decided that this particular ＿＿＿＿＿ is not for you. As promised, I enclose your refund. I very much hope we have the pleasure of supplying you soon – hopefully next time with a ＿＿＿＿＿ or other product more suited to your requirements.

Yours sincerely,

William Smith,
Customer Services Manager

A word about credit cards . . .

It is also worth mentioning that if the customer paid by credit card you can run into difficulties when they receive their credit card statement and do not recognise the purchase. This can happen if the item is listed by your company name, e.g. Smithco, and the customer remembers the item only by its description, e.g. The Rag Doll Collection. They then write to the credit card company saying that they have not made a purchase from Smithco. The problem arises because the card company write to you but give you only 10 days to provide evidence that the customer did make the purchase. If you miss the deadline, the customer is automatically refunded and your account debited!

This is very frustrating for you, especially since most people have made the purchase (otherwise how could you have obtained their credit card details?), but have simply forgotten about it. One way out is to ask the credit card company to list the item and not the company name on the statement. You will find that this does tend to jog people's memory.

The intention of this section is to emphasise the importance of product guarantees. Money lies at the root of most disagreements. By issuing a refund promptly and courteously you will avoid undignified, expensive and time-consuming exchanges with your customers. The sums involved should not materially affect the business (unless the product is completely unacceptable) and you will also gain a reputation for fair play. Far from losing a customer you may well find that they trust you sufficiently to order something else in the future. You really cannot lose.

YOUR 'HAPPY' FILE

This is undoubtedly the most rewarding aspect of customer service – the customer's vote of confidence. It is the 'public' recognition of your success at looking after people – a pat on the back if you like! And people do bother to write in and say thank you. It is really important that you keep and use these letters of praise. First, use them to motivate your staff – they also need to be thanked sometimes and given a sense of satisfaction. (After all, you normally hear from the 5 per cent who are unhappy rather than the 95 per cent who are pleased.) Second, testimonials are a brilliant form of PR/advertising and you should use them for your own promotion. They can be put to good use in many ways.

- **In PR about the company** Whenever you are writing a piece about your products/service, quote the customer letter that makes specific reference to your efficiency/ honesty/courtesy etc. Don't be shy!
- **In the advertisements themselves** If you remember back to Chapter 7 where we looked at copy-writing, we quoted a customer recommendation in the *Government Auction Handbook* advert: 'Your book was the best £12 I have ever spent.' It is a very powerful and convincing statement and you can do the same with your testimonials. But do remember to get written permission before you quote someone's comments, and describe them by their

initials, e.g. J.C. of Nottingham, so as to protect their privacy.

- **For MOPS/ASA/newspaper interviews** Obviously, I hope you are never called upon by the official bodies or the press to prove your honesty and reliability. But if it does ever happen, you can supplement your material with the contents of your happy file. It is proof indeed that you are not all bad!

Most of your customer testimonials will come of their own accord, but you can quite legitimately encourage people to write in with positive comment. We inadvertently did this while selling tomato seeds by offering £1,000 reward to the person who grew the largest tomato. The idea was that we could then put the reward into the advertising copy and hopefully increase response to the advert. It not only did that, but after the growing season we had a flood of letters from people who had grown what they thought might be the largest fruit and were eulogising over the size/taste/colour of the tomatoes! What a lovely bonus for us. We, of course, put this to further good use by making up a collage of people's comments and photos, and incorporating it into the next advertising campaign.

So be imaginative in the ways that you seek testimonials and make maximum use of this free source of advertising. Above all, remember that customer service is for your benefit as well as the customer's, so don't miss out on the opportunity.

11

ARE YOU
MAKING MONEY?

WELL ARE YOU? So many people manage to master the art of copy-writing/fulfilment etc, only to fail because they don't properly monitor the results of their advertising and have no real idea of whether or not they are making money. This is an absolutely crucial stage in mail order and luck just doesn't come into it. Your profit will depend upon your ability to record and analyse the initial advertising results, and so decide where next to run your 'campaign'.

Many people panic at this stage, believing that this is the catch to mail order, the difficult part they cannot master because they don't have a maths degree. Not so. The key to this part of the operation is attention to detail – recording results in such a way that they give you all the answers! You don't need to be particularly clever, you just have to know how to organise your information.

HOW TO RECORD
YOUR RESULTS

The results book is probably your most valuable asset and should become your bible. In it lie all the answers to your mail order success. Keep it well organised and up to date at all times. Start with a lever-arch file. If you have more than one product on offer, divide the file into sections, one for each product. Each section should have three divisions.

A top sheet

This should always be kept up at the front of the section. Essentially it is a summary sheet which gives you the daily and cumulative sales totals, the daily stock level and the number of returns. The information comes directly from the daily fulfilment sheets and should be set out on an A4 sheet (see page 184).

A   Always record the date of your sales. You need to be able to tie up this information with the dates on the banking slips.

B   It is important to know how many returns are coming in each day. They should be proportionate to the sales, i.e. the more sales you make, the more returns you should expect. But as a percentage of sales, they should not normally rise above 5 per cent. You can calculate this percentage by dividing the total number of returns by the total number of sales so far: 20/2,000 = 1 per cent returns. If the figure rises above 5 per cent, it suggests that there is something wrong with the product and you should look carefully at the reasons people are giving for the return. I should add that this figure will vary depending upon the product; for instance clothing returns are often much higher.

C   This is a handy reference as to the total product numbers sold to date and should always tie in with . . .

D + E   The stock level, which is arrived at by simply deducting the daily sales totals from the current stock figure. Don't forget to add in new stock as and when it arrives, and you also need to deduct any one-off sales, for example trade orders, which would not necessarily show up on the daily fulfilment sheets.

The Top Sheet

Product : Patchwork cushions

A Date	Returns B Daily	R/T	Sales C Daily	R/T	D/E Stock level Daily	New stock	Comments
1.2.94						1000	
2.2.94	–	–	79	79	921		
3.2.94			116	195	805		
4.2.94	2	2	205	400	600		
5.2.94	5	7	320	720	280	1000	
					1280		
6.2.94	4	11	230	950	1050		
7.2.94	7	18	150	1100	900		
8.2.94	5	23	70*	1170	830		* includes 30 sold in bulk to A. Black Ltd
		C/F		C/F	C/F		

Analysis sheets

This should also be an A4 sheet. The purpose of this sheet is to
provide you with an ongoing record of the performance of each
advertisement – the individual daily totals and the cumulative
figure. It is a compact and valuable document and is laid out in
such a way that you can immediately gauge the success/failure
of the advertisement (see page 186):

A **Name of product**   For ease of reference and in case the
sheet gets removed from its place in the file.

B **Media**   Obviously, you need to know exactly which
paper/magazine the results came from. Any sheets for the
same media but which came out on subsequent days
should be filed chronologically.

C **Code**   Apart from the media source this also tells you
which day of the week the advertisement ran, a factor
which can sometimes quite dramatically affect the results.
Always write in the date and the day of the week, again
for ease of comparison later on. Remember that your code
is very important in ensuring that results are correctly
analysed, so watch out especially for code allocation.
When you have lots of ads running, make sure that the
codes don't get confused, otherwise you might think that
an ad has been a success when it has not.

D **Size of ad**   You will later want to compare the
performance of different size ads, to see which one has
given the best relative results.

E **Costs**   This, in conjunction with D, will help you work
out which were the best advertising rates achieved and
will also allow you to judge the success of the sales. All
the above information (for points A–E) will be provided
by your advertising sales contact at the time of buying
space, or, if you are using a media buyer, on the media
amendment report/schedule/confirmation that he sends
you.

F **Sales figures**   Here you must record:

Analysis Sheet

Size of ad: 20x2 **D**   **A** Product: Ragdoll (at £14.95)

Cost £ 480 **E**   **B** media: Independent

C Code: Ind/08/01(mon)

F

| Date | No of orders | | | | Payment Rec'd | | | |
	Cash	c/c	Total	RIT	Cash	c/c	Total	RIT
04/01	1	—	1	1	14.95	—	14.95	14.95
05/01	9	2	11	12	134.55	29.90	164.45	179.40
06/01	18	5	23	35	269.10	74.75	343.85	523.25
07/01	25	8	33	68	373.75	119.60	493.35	1016.60
10/01	11	2	13	81	164.45	29.90	194.35	1210.95
11/01	5	1	6	87	74.75	14.95	89.70	1300.65
12/01	2	—	2	89	29.90	—	29.90	1330.55
13/01	1	—	1	90	14.95	—	14.95	1345.50
15/01	—	1	1	91	—	14.95	14.95	1360.45
18/01	2	—	2	93	29.90	—	29.90	1390.35
19/01	1	—	1	94	14.95	—	14.95	1405.30
21/01	1	—	1	95	14.95	—	14.95	1420.25
26/01	—	1	1	96	—	14.95	14.95	1435.20
28/01	1	—	1	97	14.95	—	14.95	1450.15

- the daily numbers of credit card and cash orders;
- the value of the orders;
- the running total of both the number of orders and their cash value.

This information should be taken directly from the daily report sheets sent in from the fulfilment house (see Chapter 9). Don't leave it – do it daily – since you have to be on top of the results at all times. Always buy the papers/magazines as soon as they come out. Check that the advertisement copy/size/code are all correct. Cut out the ad, marking on it exactly which page it was on, where on the page, for example, bottom left, bottom right etc., the content of the page, such as news, TV, sport etc., and whether it was solus (on its own on the page) or next to other ads. Then attach it to the back of the analysis sheet. You now have all the information you need to analyse the results accurately.

Miscellaneous orders

One last point. There will always be orders that come in without a code, either because the customer has heard about the product but is not responding to a specific advert, or because the ad was printed without a code (it is your responsibility, not the newspaper's). List these orders on a separate analysis sheet called 'Miscellaneous' – they are all still orders and still make a profit, so keep a record of them. For example, our miscellaneous sheet for *Health Tips* sales has taken several thousand pounds.

A cumulative results sheet

This is another straightforward layout, but one which will give you a weekly readout of the combined advertisement results and thus the overall profit/loss achieved for each product so far. It is useful because people tend to focus only on the winning ads and to ignore the ones that are losing money. The sheet is essentially a backup system designed to give the true and overall picture. Again, it is best laid out as an A4 sheet (see page 188).

Cumulative Results Sheet   w/e 07/01

Product: Cookery Book (£9.95)

Date of Ad	Media	Cost	£ Sales Total	No of items Sold	Fulfilment at £2.75/item	+/- £
20/11/93	Ind	250	626.85	63	173.25	203.60
03/01/94	Ind	250	507.45	51	140.25	117.20
17/10/93	GU	340	815.90	82	225.50	250.40
18/11/93	GU	340	746.25	75	206.25	200.00
05/01/94	D.Tel	900	577.10	58	159.50	(482.40)
02/01/94	S.Tel	900	2089.50	210	577.50	612.00
16/11/94	Times	720	1522.35	153	420.75	381.60
04/01/94	Times	720	447.75	45	123.75	(396.00)
						£ 886.40

It is helpful to keep results from each paper/magazine together, if possible in chronological order; you can then compare the performance of the ad in subsequent editions of the same paper. To work out the overall profit/loss situation, simply take the cost of the ad and of fulfilment away from the sales total (to find the cost of fulfilment, multiply the number of items sold by the cost of fulfilment per item). The figure left is your gross profit, that is to say your profit before you deduct the business overheads.

Don't forget that the cost of fulfilment must here include the unit cost of the product itself, in order to achieve a correct profit/loss figure.

If you have recorded your results accurately, the analysis becomes a lot easier and this is what we shall look at next.

ANALYSING YOUR ORDERS – WHAT THEY TELL YOU

When it comes to analysing results, real mail order experts have such highly developed instincts that they just know what is right and wrong, and trust themselves sufficiently to act upon it. But even they had to start out once with little knowledge or experience, and succeeded through years of testing, establishing formulae to gauge the advertising response and by recognising patterns within the results. And this is what you must do now. But don't worry. Far from being an instinctive approach, this part of the business is quite scientific and the principles hold true for anyone, however new to mail order. The following are the three most important areas to examine and understand:

1. First day's result

For **daily papers** this refers to the first day that the post arrives after the ad has come out and is not necessarily the day after the ad appears. Allowing for the postal system, the very fastest an order could reach you would be within one day and that would be unusual; for example, if the ad came out on a Tuesday, you would be lucky to get orders on the Wednesday. When it does happen, it can be an indication of a successful product – that is to say, people are so keen to order the product that they send off their money much more quickly.

If the advertisement first runs on a Sunday, it is unusual to get orders on the Monday, simply because there are very few Sunday postal collections! Remember also that if your ad ran on a Friday and you don't work on a Saturday, Monday morning will bring two days of post, which should be reflected in the volume of orders.

Don't worry if there is no post for the first 24 hours. Sometimes postal delays mean that you have to wait two days. You can always tell if it is a delay or just a poor response because if it is the former, no post gets through; if one product has a post and another does not, it suggests that the post is working but the product with no post is not.

Under normal circumstances you should certainly see the first orders on the second day after advertising. It is impossible to say exactly how many items of post to expect from the first response. It depends entirely upon the circulation of the paper. Theoretically, the larger the circulation and readership, the more people should order. Against this, of course, you will probably have paid more for a larger circulation paper and will need a greater response to make money. If, on the other hand, you have bought the ad very cheaply, you will need fewer orders to make a profit. There is no particular formula to apply at this stage – that comes into use during the next few days. We have had everything from 0–100 orders from a first day's post; you just have to wait and see what the next few days bring to really judge.

Magazine and periodical response is somewhat different. It is much harder to anticipate the first day's response, as the publication date is not as rigid as it would be with a daily or weekly newspaper. Many magazines actually come out two weeks before the month printed on the cover, i.e. a May edition might come out on 14 April. Response may take a few days to filter through, especially as people buy their monthly magazines at varying times of the month. So don't expect quite the same pattern of response as you would get with a daily paper. One thing you must do is get your voucher copy as soon as possible after publication date, just to make sure that it really did come out, correctly coded etc. Then you can relax a little and wait for the orders to come in.

2. First week's result

Now you can start to work out whether or not you are going to make money. With daily papers the first five days' results will give enough information to gauge the overall performance of the advertisement. Depending upon which day of the week your ad came out, there are different ways of calculating your likely end result.

- If the ad came out on a Saturday or a Sunday, you should multiply by two the sales achieved by the following Friday to find out what your eventual sales figure is likely to be:

Sat Sun	Mon	Tues	Wed	Thurs	Fri	
Ad comes out	0	5	10	19	32	**No of orders**

Your final result will probably be something in the region of 132 orders   −   i.e.
$2 \times (\text{Mon} + \text{Tues} + \text{Wed} + \text{Thurs} + \text{Fri}) = 2 \times 66 = \underline{\underline{132}}.$

- If the ad came out on a weekday, you should multiply by two only the first three days' post, to gauge your likely end result:

Mon	Tues	Wed	Thurs	
Ad comes out	4	12	16	$= 2 \times 32 = \underline{\underline{64}}.$

But are you making a profit?

Having worked that out, you then need to know if that volume of sales is sufficient to make a profit. In the book business, because of the particular margins we work on (sometimes as much as 80 per cent), we know that any ad which brings in revenue of more than two times the advertisement cost is making money, and three and four times ad cost is considered an excellent result. This two times formula can be applied to any product with an 80 per cent margin, i.e. where the sales price of the item is five times the cost price. If your profit margin is at the lower end recommended for mail order products, i.e. 66 per cent (a 3:1 sales:cost price ratio), you would need three times the ad cost to make money.

The main exception to this rule is for those products sold up front at no profit, but which have follow on products carrying a high profit margin, for example, halogen lamps sold at cost price needing bulbs costing £7 each. Here you could afford to see less than a two or three times return on the initial ad, because you are going to make money on follow-up sales.

The break-even formula

Alternatively, you can work out exactly how many items need to be sold to make a profit by dividing the cost of the advert by the profit margin on each item. This tells you what your break-even point is. If you have an item with a £2 profit margin and an ad that cost £500, you will need to sell 250 items to cover costs. Obviously, this is your minimum target – actually to make money you will need to sell more than 250 items, especially when you consider the following:

- Not every ad will make a profit and the losses will negate the gains made by the winners.
- The profit at this stage is actually just the gross profit, as you still have to cover overheads – rent, rates, telephone, stationery, accountants, wages etc. Your real profit is what is left after all these deductions. This is your operating

profit. Clearly when you start out you can and should use the formulae given above to gauge your gross profit. Your operating profit will depend upon the frequency and success of the ads, that is to say, whether or not at the end of the year the profit made on individual ads will add up to more than the cost of your overheads. This is not something you can know in advance, but your skill in deciding when and when not to rebook individual ads will ensure that your day-to-day performance is under control and that the end of year figure is a positive one.

3. Patterns of response

So, now you know how to calculate what your sales levels need to be on a per ad basis. But you should also be able to recognise patterns within the results, so that you can differentiate between what is good and bad.

Newspapers

A newspaper advert will usually reach its peak sales level on day four or five, hover there for a day or two, then decline slowly. The pattern might look like this:

Day	No of orders
1	5
2	11
3	20
4	27
5	23
6	18
7	12
8	5
9	3
10	1
11	2

Orders can continue to come in ones and twos for several months. Don't underestimate the effect of the last few stragglers. On weaker ads it can mean the difference between breaking even and losing money. So record every order, right up to the very last one.

Magazines

Results from magazines and any publication with shelf-life come in slowly over a period of months, sometimes even years. But before you have visions of yourself growing old waiting for the orders to show up, be advised that 90 per cent of the orders should arrive within the first month of publication.

How quickly do people respond?

There is rhyme and reason to the overall pattern. With newspaper ads the majority of customers will be decisive and order within the first few days. The rest will take longer for a variety of reasons; some people sit on the ad, hesitating until subsequent ads reinforce their desire, prompt them to dig out the original coupon and react; sometimes the paper will end up in a doctor's waiting-room; sometimes it gets sent overseas to expats; and occasionally people just forget, only to find the torn-out advertisement behind the sofa some weeks later. Despite the arbitrary nature of these examples, this pattern of peak and trough is surprisingly consistent, regardless of ad size, cost of product etc. This consistency is very much a good thing as it helps you to know what to expect once the ad has come out.

Once again, magazines are slightly different. Because they don't date as quickly as a daily paper, people don't feel under the same pressure to respond to the ads. They are often left lying around in waiting-rooms or kept by the purchaser. The response is accordingly slower and somewhat more sporadic, although it will always tail off in much the same way as a newspaper ad would, but over a longer period of time.

Remember, only very successful products will encourage people to divert from the norm and react more quickly. You should therefore be suspicious of the following:

- **Inconsistent results** That is to say, nothing for the first few day and then 20 orders suggests that the post has been held up. Or a sudden resurgence in the results when the ad looked as if it was tailing off suggests that the codes have been confused and the figures misallocated.
- **Results stopping dead** In 'real life' this just doesn't happen – results always tail off gently. Again, check your code.
- **No result at all** There is a minute possibility that if you had a badly written advertisement for a poor product in a small circulation paper you might get no response at all. But it would be extremely unusual and has certainly never happened in my experience. Even my biggest flop – a book about self-defence for women – managed one solitary order! It is much more likely that your advertisement has no code and that your results have been posted under 'miscellaneous'.

CAPITALISING UPON SUCCESS

So, you have run an advertisement which has done better than break even and made some profit. That is what you set out to do. Now you need to know how to make the most of it. Your next step is to extend the advertising, concentrating on two specific areas.

1. Rebooking the same media

If an advertisement has worked once you would be foolish not to repeat it in the same media. It is obviously the safest place to start as you have already proved that it does well for your product. But the frequency with which you do so will make a big difference to your results, and will vary depending upon the type of product being sold and the media used. Basically, you have a choice between taking a long and short-term approach to the advertising campaign.

The short-term view

You might decide to repeat the ad every couple of weeks (or monthly in the case of a magazine) and squeeze out the profits as quickly as possible. This is fine (for as long as the ad is making money) and will suit any item with a novelty value or any product where you fear swift competition. But you have to accept that public interest will fizzle out pretty quickly and you will have to find another product to sell. This may suit you if the business is just part-time, but anyone in it long-term will need a constant supply of new ideas. Having said that, there is nothing wrong with a short, sharp injection of profit. Some of our books are very much novelty titles, such as *How To Talk to Your Cat*, and although our campaign only lasted four months, we sold almost 55,000 copies of the book in that time!

If you take the short-term view you also have to take into account the readership profile of the media being used. Most national newspapers have a fairly consistent readership and you cannot therefore repeat the same ad more than about once a fortnight – otherwise you are aiming at the same people who are obviously not going to buy the same product twice! But this is not the case for all media; *Loot*, for example, is a London-based daily paper which advertises items for sale. People tend to buy the paper occasionally and when they are looking for a specific item. As a result, different people read *Loot* every day. Here you could happily run an advert on consecutive days and get a new response each time.

The long-term view

You may decide, however, to opt for a long-term advertising campaign. This tends to suit products with more lasting value and appeal, e.g. a dinner service, clothes, reference books etc., items that will sell almost regardless of the time of year. In a perfect world every mail order business would have at least one of these products, simply because they can tide you over when things are otherwise slow. In this instance you should repeat the ad no more than once a month in order to keep it fresh and you will find that the product can last for up to a year or even longer.

Know when to stop

Whichever approach you choose, the golden rule is to stop advertising the minute an ad stops making money. Unless you have a very good reason for thinking that it was a freak result, such as the weather, politics, post etc., don't be tempted to try 'just once more' because your losses will very quickly negate any previous profit. Moreover, when you rebook an ad use the same copy as before. Don't try to change something that works! You might not be able to get exactly the same position on the page, but at least you haven't jeopardised the result by indulging a whim and substituting a new headline.

2. Trying other media

You will also want to spread out and try to repeat your success with different media. There are several factors to consider here.

Where to book the ad

Again, this largely depends upon the product. For those with wide-ranging or more upmarket appeal, you should keep to the upper market papers that you started with (see Chapter 8), then try middle market and finally move to mass market papers. Be aware that the mass market is potentially the most profitable area because of the huge circulation of those papers (see table in Chapter 8), but are usually the hardest to crack! This is because people who read mass market papers are often from a lower income bracket and less disposed to risk what they have. The overriding rule is to move first to the paper/magazine closest in profile to the one you have successfully tested. Move slowly and cautiously. For example, if you were advertising in the *Independent* and it worked, try the *Guardian* next, then the *Observer* and

Telegraph, and lastly the *Sun* and the *Daily Mirror*. I would not just leap from the *Independent* to the *Sun* – the gap is too wide.

Your readership profile

Very much the same rules apply here as for choosing your initial advertisement. If your product was specific in that it aimed at a particular age range, for example, a book about retirement, or was a niche item, such as a collection of first edition stamps, select the media with the most suitable profile; the *Daily Telegraph* and the *Observer* are both suitable upmarket papers, but the *Telegraph* has a slightly older readership and might be better for a publication on retirement. You could try to sell the stamps through specialist and collectors magazines. It is really a question of matching the product with the most suitable media, although the most popular products will succeed almost anywhere. But such products only turn up once every few years! For the rest of the time, you will have to analyse your market carefully so as not to make expensive mistakes.

How often to book the ad

This is just a question of starting again with a first advertisement and then, according to your objectives and the initial response, repeating the advertisement fortnightly or monthly. It is exactly the same procedure as outlined above.

How much to pay

The first flush of success is a dangerous thing, because you can easily get carried away and start booking adverts regardless of the cost, thinking that the product will make money. The simple rule is that you cannot afford to pay more than the minimum! This is the basis upon which you have made money first time round, and the delicate balance of ad/product/fulfilment cost must be maintained, even more so because subsequent advertisements will eventually attract less response. As we discussed in Chapter 8, you should aim to pay no more than 50 per cent of rate card and hopefully less. Don't budge from that figure. And stop advertising the minute an ad stops making money.

How much space to take

This is another area where you can easily undo all the good work if you are not very careful. You will have started advertising with a fractional advertisement, one that takes up only a small part of the whole page. You might be tempted to try a larger space in the hope that more people will notice the advert and respond. That is, of course, possible but since you cannot control the page number or page position, your larger ad might just end up in a very poor position and actually do worse because of it. For some products, particularly those which need an illustration, a large space might be necessary. Generally speaking though, it is the strength of your headline and copy-writing that will sell the product, more so than the ad size. Remember, too, that larger advertisements will cost more, if only on a pro rata basis, so there is slightly more at risk.

One area that does work well is that of Sunday colour supplement magazine full-page adverts. This is undoubtedly where the real volume of mail order business lies. But it only works with an extremely successful product and when you are paying much less than rate card; the difference might be between paying £5,000 and £15,000 – and that is what allows you to make your profit. You can, none the less, see that even the cheap rate is a lot of money. Making a mistake at this level can wipe out months of profit, so steer away from full-page advertising until you are experienced and confident – leave it to the professionals to take the risks. Most people have to feel their way, so don't bet what you can't afford to lose.

THE MOST COMMON REASONS BEHIND FAILURE

Quite apart from the product itself, there are a number of reasons why an advertisement might not pull in a good response. Most of these reasons are avoidable, so take a look at this checklist before you book any space.

Wrong media

Make sure that your product is advertised in a medium read by the most relevant age/socio-economic group and if pertinent, by the right sex. Use *BRAD*.

Wrong price

Never think that you have to pay rate card. First, you can't afford to: most mail order businesses would have a hard time making money if they had to pay rate card. Second, there are always deals available, especially if you are prepared to wait; don't ever feel pressurised into taking space – the only 'right time' to buy is when it is being offered at the right price.

Wrong time of year

This is very much common sense – you wouldn't try to sell beachware in the depths of winter. If you are in any doubt, look at other mail order advertisements – what are they selling? If you can't see anything even remotely resembling your product being advertised there is probably a very good reason why.

Wrong position within the media

This might mean that you are on the wrong page, such as the sports page when you are advertising a dried flower arrangement or on the wrong part of the page, for example, at the bottom, wedged between larger advertisements. If you are taking advantage of cheap space you do have to take pot luck to some extent, but you can stipulate that you want the first half of the paper, TV page etc. and not, for instance, business or sport.

It is in the newspaper's interest to try and accommodate you, because if the ad doesn't work you won't buy again!

Product priced incorrectly

Product pricing is covered in Chapter 4. You have to strike a balance between:

- what is commercially viable, i.e. what will make you a profit;
- what the market will bear, i.e. what the customer is prepared to pay;
- what other people are charging for similar products.

You can actually charge too little as well as too much; quite apart from the economics involved we know that we couldn't sell a book on health for under £5 as it would simply lack credibility in the customer's eyes. On the other hand you have to be aware of the customer's psychological price barriers; £9.95 always sounds better than £10. Remember also, that you cannot easily price-test in the papers.

Unconvincing body copy

Before you pay for an advertisement, read through what you have written and ask other people to do so as well. The simple rule is – 'If you are not convinced by the advertisement, nobody else will be!'

Headline needs changing

Even the most brilliant body copy is useless if the headline hasn't grabbed the reader's attention. Those first few words can make or break your advertisements. You may not be allowed to play around with price, but you can and should test headlines. Our *Health Tips* book is one of our bestsellers, but it only started to do well when we changed the headline from *Health Remedies*. Just one word made all the difference: 'Tips' sounds light, easy to understand, something you can dip into; 'Remedies' sounds a bit old-fashioned, heavy going and suggests that the cure may be less than pleasant! So do keep changing your headline until you find a winner.

Incorrect code

The importance of coding cannot be emphasised enough. Unless you have a specific agreement with the newspaper/media buyer, the responsibility for delivering correctly coded copy is yours. If a newspaper offers to set the ad, ask to see a proof before it goes to print. Make sure the code is clear and easily visible – otherwise you will slow down the fulfilment process. Pay great attention to these details; they can seriously affect your campaign (please see page 107).

Incorrect response mechanism

You need to check two things:

- Have you told the customer exactly what to pay and where to send the order to?
- Have you asked them for their name, address and postcode so that you can fulfil the order in return?

It may sound unlikely, but I have seen national newspaper advertisements by well-known companies that failed to give proper addresses or enough room for the customer to fill in their details. I have organised hundreds of advertisements, but even we let one through recently that forgot to mention how much the book cost! Red faces all round. So do check – I couldn't bear to think that there may be people eager to put their cheque in the post but with no address to send it to!

Weather/politics . . .

These rogue factors were mentioned in Chapter 8 and short of having a hotline to the Met Office and the services of a prophet, there is little you can do about these events. But you can take comfort from the fact that it is rare for them to completely disrupt business.

12

EXPANDING

THE

BUSINESS

I N THIS BOOK I have concentrated on the use of magazine and newspaper advertisements to establish your mail order business. In your first few months of trading you will be devoting all your resources to just getting the enterprise on its feet. Once you make a profit your thoughts will turn towards expansion and how to capitalise upon your early work. This can be done in several ways: selling again to established customers, finding new customers and making money from the rental of your own customer names. This last area is potentially very profitable and very much the icing on the mail order cake. If you can get this far there are great opportunities to make extra money without too much extra effort.

EXTENDING YOUR
PRODUCT RANGE

First you have to know how to create new products, as well as make the most of the ones you already have. Without these tools you have nothing to offer either existing or potential customers. There are basically two ways to extend your product range.

Extend a single product line

It could be hand-painted boxes or tomato seeds, but the principle is the same. Extend the range and offer a series of differently decorated boxes, or miniature tomatoes as well as giant ones, i.e you sell basically the same thing, but with slight variations. What you are trying to do is capture a greater proportion of a proven market. You have found that people like hand-painted boxes, so it is logical to assume that a series of them will appeal to both old and new customers. But there must be a new element to the product, or you will find that you have simply exhausted current demand rather than created a new one.

Add different items on a similar theme

Equally, you can develop the theme of your product. If you started by offering a book on golf, you could introduce golf ball paperweights, golfing clothes, golfing mugs, hats, the list is endless. We followed up our giant tomato campaign with an offer for giant vegetables. Of course, some of our customers were only interested in tomatoes, but quite a few just wanted to grow large vegetables, and went on to buy pumpkins, onions, leeks and radishes. Our first health book sold well. So we built up a library of health titles: *Arthritis, Irritable Bowel Syndrome, Impotence* etc. Lakeland Plastics started out by selling plastic bags to the mail order market. They have since expanded this to an enormous range of catering and kitchen equipment, mostly by asking the customers what *they* want to buy.

Finding completely new products

From time to time you will want to introduce a completely new product. That is fine, but do make sure that it has passed the analysis test laid out in Chapter 3. Don't take unnecessary risks, and wherever possible go with something that has a proven track record.

TRADING THROUGHOUT THE YEAR

This method of expansion can also help you to maintain a consistent volume of business throughout the year. If you want to work seasonally this will not apply. But many of you will hope to build up an ongoing mail order business and one that provides an income each month. Different products will appeal to different times of the year. The golfing book would sell well before Christmas, while golfing clothes would do well in the spring and summer. Moreover, people begin to look out for your ads, since they start to see you as 'the golf specialist'. You are beginning to build an identity for your little empire! Past Times redressed the balance of their Christmas orientated items by introducing a gardening gift line, geared towards the spring.

YOUR STOCK LEVELS

At this point it is also worth giving some thought to your stock levels and storage facilities. Don't fall into the trap of overextending yourself and purchasing too much stock. Only expand by one item at a time and test each product (as you did your first) with a small quantity of stock before building a full-blown campaign. Go slowly. It is generally unwise to leap from one product straight to a group of five or six. You will tie up too much cash in stock, spend large amounts on testing and have no guarantee that any of the new items will sell. Even if one does, it may not cover the losses made on the four that didn't. If you were lucky enough to succeed earlier on it does not mean that you can now throw caution to the wind. Test one new product at a time and settle for being restrained but solvent!

WORKING YOUR BACKLIST

Never neglect your backlist – an excellent way to extend the life of your product range and one that is sadly under-explored in many businesses. 'Backlist' is technically a publishing term and refers to old titles – books that sold one or two years previously and then gradually declined in popularity. However, it can equally apply to any company's list of past products. Never ignore these items. There isn't much new in this world and many products are cyclical. Unless you specialise in fads, the likelihood is that your backlist still has some life left in it.

Make a point of re-testing these products at least once a year. Timing is very important here. These products will almost certainly not last as long as they did the first time round. You have to know when to stop advertising because when they stop selling the second or third time round, it tends to happen very suddenly and without warning. Don't therefore commit yourself to more than one ad at a time. The minute the orders appear to be slowing down, stop the advertising. Otherwise, you could lose your shirt.

Armed with both a backlist and new products, you can now set about increasing your sales levels.

SELLING AGAIN TO
ESTABLISHED CUSTOMERS

This is an excellent and cost-effective way of increasing your sales levels, and is fundamental to the growth and success of your business. You have an enormous advantage here. These are people who already know and trust you. They have already bought once so you know that they are interested in a certain type of product. If your product and service have been good they will be quite prepared to look at whatever else you are offering. These customer names are just about the best prospect you have, so you have to maximise your sales with these people.

The Royal Mail estimates that it is up to three times as effective to mail to these people as it is mailing to a list from another source. Companies like Unwins Seeds know that their real business comes from cultivating long-term customers. This can be done in two ways.

- **By inserts** These are normally A4 or A5 sized sheets advertising your product, typically with a letter to the customer on one side, and the advertisement and response mechanism on the other.
- **By catalogues** They are convenient when you have built up a variety of products and cannot list them easily on one or two sheets.

Both inserts and catalogues can be sent to the customer with their initial order and/or subsequently at intervals. In Chapter 10, we looked at one way of increasing sales in between receiving the initial order and fulfilling it. Here we are extending the same principle. The expensive part of mail order is identifying and capturing the customer; that is to say, on your initial sale you have had to cover the cost of advertising (as well as all other direct costs). Now you know who is interested in your products you should try to sell to them again. This time round your profit margin shoots up because you have eliminated the advertising costs. All you pay for is the production of the inserts/ catalogues, and in some instances envelopes and stamps as well. You will sometimes hear these sales methods referred to as 'bounce backs'.

Inserts

You can either slip your insert in with the initial fulfilment or start a regular mailing to all past customers. Generally speaking, the sooner you follow up with another offer the more success you are likely to have. The customer is still 'hot', still in the mood to buy and fired up by the first offer. Move in and entice them with a second. You can make the offer as detailed as you like. One of the advantages of this form of direct mail is that you aren't confined to the size of a newspaper advertisement. This gives you greater flexibility as to the type of products you can follow up with; if they would benefit from a more detailed description, there is nothing to stop you including it.

For most single items, I would recommend an A5/A4 sheet with a letter to the customer on one side and an advertisement on the other. The rules for writing the ad are no different from those given in Chapter 7. Since you have more space to play with, you should consider including a response coupon – it just makes it that bit easier for the customer to order. The letter need not be very complicated and can be simply laid out on your headed notepaper. The key to this letter is to draw out the product benefits and reiterate them. Look at the example (pages 210–211) – not a long letter by mail order standards, in fact, but it still manages to summarise neatly the reasons why the customer should buy the product.

If you are sending out to less than 100 people, you could probably get away with typing and photocopying. Otherwise, you should have your letter professionally printed. Unless your product requires a photo or coloured illustration, it is quite acceptable to use simple black print on white paper. Your layout should be clear and easy to follow. Glossy productions may *look* impressive, but they are expensive. Moreover, unless the copy is good they still won't convince the reader to buy. The customer wants to think that they are getting a good deal and fancy paper may make them slightly suspicious of your costs.

Make a point of noting those people who buy again. You can either do this manually or on your computer. Flag (mark) their names each time they purchase another product, noting what they bought, when they bought it and how much they spent. The more often they buy, the more valuable those names become – both to you and anyone who wants subsequently to rent your names (more about this later). A regular mail order purchaser is someone worth cultivating!

Dear Customer,

Welcome to Marshalls 1989 Catalogue . . .
. . . A Treasure House of Superb Quality Seeds

Firstly, may I say what a pleasure it is for me to write this letter of welcome to introduce the New Season's Marshalls Catalogue to valued customers like yourself. It's an opportunity also for me to tell you about developments here at Wisbech, especially the new varieties we're adding to the catalogue.

More Marshalls Firsts . . . New Vegetable Varieties . . .
. . . With Class, Quality and Taste

Our trials and research have continued to identify varieties which offer significant improvements in yield, consistency, harvesting and quality of taste. Both at home and on the trial grounds, our labours in proving new varieties have shown some very commendable results. It's a very special moment for me when I can confirm that we've another winner that's worthy of being featured in our catalogue.

I won't mention my favourites right now. But I have made a few notes at the bottom of the next page, which I hope you'll find invaluable as you plan your seed order.

New Flowers from Marshalls . . . For Brighter Beds and Borders

You know — some of these newer flower seed varieties really are jolly good. Time and time again they show their worth. There's no doubt that careful breeding produces stronger, more vigorous plants with earlier flowering, extended flowering and better resistance to disease and weather. I suggest you keep your eye open for the Fleuroselect symbol — 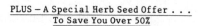 it's the sign of a 5 Star Flower.

If you want to have a go at the really new varieties, take note from my list overleaf — they're bloomin' marvels.

PLUS — A Special Herb Seed Offer . . .
To Save You Over 50%

We sometimes forget these days about cutting herbs from the garden. Fresh herbs make such a difference in good home cooking. So what better than a half price offer to establish your own herb bed, with heady scents in the

S. E. Marshall & Co. Ltd.,
Wisbech, Cambridgeshire PE13 2RF
Telephone: Wisbech (0945) 583407

This direct mail letter highlights plenty of benefits for the customer

garden and great flavours in the kitchen. Just send an order for £20 or
more and I'll add our special collection of 14 different varieties for
just £2.95. That's about half what you can normally expect to pay.

<u>Prompt Customer Service and Delivery Service . . .</u>
<u>. . . That Other Seedsmen Envy!</u>

Something you can continue to be sure of with Marshalls, is that we pride
ourselves in giving better service than any other seed firm. This year
we're working even harder to offer 24 hour despatch on telephone orders —
so if you need urgent delivery now or want to place a quick top-up order
during the season, give us a call with your credit card order.

May I wish you a very happy 1989, and a successful year in your garden
with Marshalls Seeds.

Best Wishes,

John Kierman.

John Kierman
General Manager

PS — Don't forget to order your Seed Potatoes and Onion Sets NOW with
your main seed order. It can save you time and postage. We won't hold your
seed order up. If necessary we'll send separate shipments of these items
later at our expense.

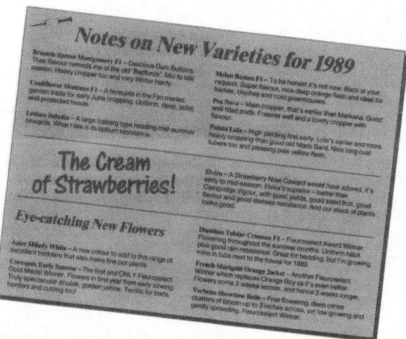

Catalogues

Catalogues only apply when you have built up a variety of products and cannot fit them comfortably on the single A4 sheet. As with inserts, you can send one out with the initial order or at subsequent intervals. The layout should again be kept simple. We design ours with a front page covering letter, the ads on the inside pages and order form on the back cover. The adverts are written in exactly the same way as those we place in the media, but the response mechanism is replaced by the order form. You should get this professionally typeset and printed. Below is an

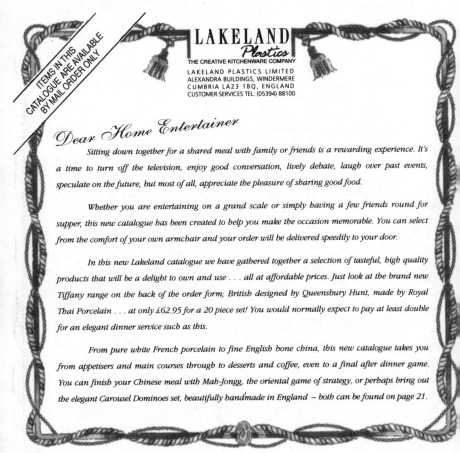

ITEMS IN THIS CATALOGUE ARE AVAILABLE BY MAIL ORDER ONLY

LAKELAND *Plastics*
THE CREATIVE KITCHENWARE COMPANY
LAKELAND PLASTICS LIMITED
ALEXANDRA BUILDINGS, WINDERMERE
CUMBRIA LA23 1BQ, ENGLAND
CUSTOMER SERVICES TEL: (05394) 88100

Dear Home Entertainer

Sitting down together for a shared meal with family or friends is a rewarding experience. It's a time to turn off the television, enjoy good conversation, lively debate, laugh over past events, speculate on the future, but most of all, appreciate the pleasure of sharing good food.

Whether you are entertaining on a grand scale or simply having a few friends round for supper, this new catalogue has been created to help you make the occasion memorable. You can select from the comfort of your own armchair and your order will be delivered speedily to your door.

In this new Lakeland catalogue we have gathered together a selection of tasteful, high quality products that will be a delight to own and use . . . all at affordable prices. Just look at the brand new Tiffany range on the back of the order form; British designed by Queensbury Hunt, made by Royal Thai Porcelain . . . at only £62.95 for a 20 piece set! You would normally expect to pay at least double for an elegant dinner service such as this.

From pure white French porcelain to fine English bone china, this new catalogue takes you from appetisers and main courses through to desserts and coffee, even to a final after dinner game. You can finish your Chinese meal with Mah-Jongg, the oriental game of strategy, or perhaps bring out the elegant Carousel Dominoes set, beautifully handmade in England – both can be found on page 21.

example from Lakeland Plastics.

If you are thinking about colour pictures, get professional help with the design. With a simple catalogue format you can draw it up first long-hand and ask the printer to work from this.

The order form is very important. If you are offering several items, you should try and get the customer to buy more than one at a time. Apart from the postage, your fulfilment costs are practically the same whether the customer buys one or a few items. Once again, your profit margin goes up. You should therefore try to encourage the customer to make a multiple purchase by offering some sort of discount, free gift and/or free

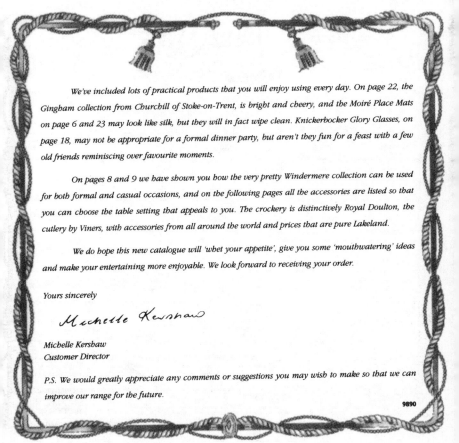

We've included lots of practical products that you will enjoy using every day. On page 22, the Gingham collection from Churchill of Stoke-on-Trent, is bright and cheery, and the Moiré Place Mats on page 6 and 23 may look like silk, but they will in fact wipe clean. Knickerbocker Glory Glasses, on page 18, may not be appropriate for a formal dinner party, but aren't they fun for a feast with a few old friends reminiscing over favourite moments.

On pages 8 and 9 we have shown you how the very pretty Windermere collection can be used for both formal and casual occasions, and on the following pages all the accessories are listed so that you can choose the table setting that appeals to you. The crockery is distinctively Royal Doulton, the cutlery by Viners, with accessories from all around the world and prices that are pure Lakeland.

We do hope this new catalogue will 'whet your appetite', give you some 'mouthwatering' ideas and make your entertaining more enjoyable. We look forward to receiving your order.

Yours sincerely

Michelle Kershaw

Michelle Kershaw
Customer Director

P.S. We would greatly appreciate any comments or suggestions you may wish to make so that we can improve our range for the future.

9890

postage and packing. Notice how the Lakeland Plastics order
form (below) offers free postage and packing for orders over
£30.00. Notice also their unconditional guarantee.

Remember your direct costs and don't offer so big a discount
that you actually erode your profit margin. Remember, too,
those psychological price barriers I mentioned. If, for example,
your products are £12.95 each, you might offer two for £22.94,
three for £32.95 and four for £39.95. This would always depend
upon the cost price of the product, but generally speaking the
discount is loaded at the top end and should preferably be easy
to compare with the single unit price. A figure of £39.95 for four

---

OUR GUARANTEE
"Satisfied" is not good enough for Lakeland.
We want you to be delighted! If not, we will gladly
replace any item or give you a full refund.
(This is in addition to your statutory rights.)

LAKELAND
Plastics
THE CREATIVE KITCHENWARE COMPANY
LAKELAND PLASTICS LIMITED, ALEXANDRA BUILDINGS, WINDERMERE
CUMBRIA LA23 1BQ, ENGLAND. CUSTOMER SERVICES TEL: (05394) 88100

ORDER FORM
Please send this complete page in the
reply envelope provided
If you would like your parcel sent to an address different from
that given opposite, or if your address has changed, please
write delivery/correct address* here (*delete as necessary).

PLEASE REMEMBER TO FILL IN YOUR NAME & ADDRESS. (BLOCK CAPITALS PLEASE). **HE1**

Mr/Mrs/Miss/Ms _____

House No. & Street _____

Town _____ County _____

Postcode _____ Tel (inc. STD) _____

Mr/Mrs/Miss/Ms _____

House No. & Street _____

Town _____

County _____

Postcode _____ Tel (inc. STD) _____

CATALOGUE REF NO.	NO. OF PACKS OR ITEMS	PRODUCT DESCRIPTION	PRICE £	p

IMPORTANT NOTICE
It may be necessary to adjust price or
quantities in the event of an increase in
VAT rates or as the result of an international
price increase. Customers are entitled to a
full refund if this is not acceptable.

I enclose my cheque/postal order for

£ _____
(payable to Lakeland Plastics Limited)

Please allow 10 days for delivery

Please add Postage, Packing & Insurance (UK only)
For orders up to £29.99:............................£2.25
For orders over £30.00: ....POST FREE
These rates apply to each individual delivery address.
Please debit my credit card account

Access ☐   Visa ☐   Mastercard ☐

No. ☐☐☐☐ ☐☐☐☐ ☐☐☐☐ ☐☐☐☐
Card Expiry Date

_____/_____ Signature_____
If paying by credit card, the cardholder's address must be shown above.

	TOTAL
Postage, Packing & Insurance	
GRAND TOTAL	

*THANK YOU
SO MUCH FOR
YOUR ORDER*

USE YOUR CREDIT CARD
TO ORDER

REMEMBER WHEN YOU PAY BY ACCESS OR VISA YOUR ACCOUNT IS NOT DEBITED BY US UNTIL WE HAVE DESPATCHED YOUR ORDER

items is quite tempting when the single unit price is £12.95 – that's one free! If an item isn't selling well, drop it immediately.

Don't forget that the weight of a catalogue might push your postage up to the next band. Bear this in mind if sending it out with the initial order.

Lastly, keep a record of those customers who order from your catalogue mailing, as they are worth sending out to with further offers. For reasons of economy, don't keep sending to those who haven't made a purchase after, say, a year of mailings.

SELLING TO NEW CUSTOMERS

Reselling to established customers is an excellent way to make good profit margins. But if your business is to expand in the long term, you also need to find new customers. We have already looked at one aspect of this – whenever you build up an advertising campaign you are selling the same product but to new people – however, there are other ways, as shown below.

Renting mailing lists

With the exception of display advertising, this is potentially the most versatile and targeted way of sourcing new customers, both to sell new products and to squeeze more sales out of something previously offered through press advertisements. Mailing lists were not included earlier on in the book as they don't have quite as wide an application as newspaper or magazine advertising; mailing lists are relatively expensive to use and are therefore most often used for more expensive products, say £30 upwards. Having said that, if your product is a strong one it will always stand a good chance of making money through lists; the *Government Auction Handbook* actually started life being sold this way and did very well, despite the relatively low price of £12.95. So mailing lists are worth looking at.

What is a mailing list?

A mailing list is a database of names and addresses of people. The main theme of this is often a product that they have purchased, such as clothes, sports equipment, a car etc. It can also be a particular set of features, that is to say, people who play golf, take foreign holidays, work in computer management, or subscribe to a magazine or service. By being able to identify individuals this closely, anyone writing to them with an offer of a similar or related item will obviously stand a much greater chance of making a sale.

Mailing lists also have the advantage of allowing you to test a product away from the prying eyes of competitors, something you cannot avoid with newspaper advertising. Moreover, you are often targeting the customer at home, where they do not feel pressurised and have time to read your material. Even when targeting business people, they are in an environment conducive to considering your proposal. Mailing lists have become big business and there are scores of companies offering lists of every possible customer profile you could imagine.

How do I find the right list?

The best approach for a beginner is as follows.

- Obtain a copy of *BRAD's Direct Marketing*. *BRAD* gives details of lists by category, e.g. book buyers, clothing buyers etc., and you should look for the one with the closest affinity to your product. You then contact direct the company named as handling the list.
- Contact the Direct Marketing Association (details at the back of the book) who will be able to supply you with the names of member list brokers. These are companies who look after/rent out lists on behalf of the list owner. Mardev and Dudley Jenkins are currently the largest operators in

the UK (addresses at the back of this book). The list broker will be able to give you details of the names they manage. Don't be afraid to make use of their expertise – give them a full brief of what you want to sell and let them suggest a suitable list.

• Contact the list owner direct. This can be any organisation whose database of customers you think would match your product. It could be a magazine's list of subscribers or a furniture company's list of recent purchasers. If they are handling their names 'in-house', they may not have quite the same technology as a list broker. Against that, there is always the chance that the names have not been so heavily marketed and are quite fresh.

Whichever source you rent from, make sure that you choose the right list for your needs by asking the following questions.

1. How were the lists compiled (i.e. what is the source of the names)?
2. How recently were the lists compiled?
3. Are they updated? If so, how often? (Old names, i.e. more than one year, are usually less responsive.)
4. Who else has used the list? (To help you assess its suitability for your product.)
5. Has the list been de-duped? (That is to say, each name should only appear once on the list.)
6. How many of the people are named? (As opposed to just 'The Householder', 52 Park Road, etc.)
7. Is the list registered under the Data Protection Act? (See Chapter 6.)
8. If a consumer list, has it been MPS cleaned? (The Mailing Preference Service issues its members with the names of people who do not want to receive direct mail or are willing to receive only specific subject matter.)
9. Is the list suitable for your target group?

Once you have chosen a list, the list owner will want to see a sample of your material to make sure that it doesn't conflict with their own interests and is decent/legal etc. Once that has been accepted, start discussing the rental price. Don't just accept the first price quoted, always negotiate; explain that you are starting up, may well rent large volumes of names but want to test first. Tempt the broker/list owner with the promise of business to come, very much the way you would when buying advertising space.

What will it cost?

Prices quoted will vary, depending upon the specialisation and rarity of the names. A list of people living in Yorkshire would cost less than a list of those living in Yorkshire, on a salary of £15,000 per annum, who have bought a car within the last 12 months. The better quality and more specific the list, the more it will cost. Expect to pay between £50 and £125 per 1,000 names (1993/4 prices). You will be charged extra for any special 'selections' you may make, such as stipulating only the female names from a list or only those living in London. You will also be charged approximately £6 per 1,000 for adhesive address labels and approximately £20 per 1,000 delivery charges. The total cost of renting 1,000 names will normally be around £100; most people start by testing between 1,000 and 5,000 names. Remember that this doesn't include the cost of printing the inserts/catalogues, envelopes and postage fees. It only allows you to mail out on a one-off basis and most firms plant dummy names in the list to make sure that you don't mail out twice.

Testing

Don't ever commit to a large number of names until you have tried the first batch and found them to be successful. You then need to test different advertising material, to see which approach sells the product most successfully. The most important lesson to remember when testing is to test only one thing at a time.

You might want to try two different headlines, dividing your names into two groups. That's fine, but don't do it while also testing the impact of, for example, an illustration against the straightforward printed word. If response increases, you won't know which element was responsible! In the same vein, always send out your mailshot from the same place on the same day. You might think that splitting your mailshot between two different days can't make a difference – but the FA Cup or a bomb blast could seriously affect response. There are also daily and seasonal variations to consider. For consumer mailings it is often a good idea to time the mailing so that it arrives on a Saturday, when many people are at home with more time to read the literature. Equally, it is a bad idea to send out a mailshot in August, when many families are away on holiday. Whichever, the aim is to work out the best package and to use this as your 'control' – until you next make changes and improvements.

Testing also allows you to experiment with 'one stage' versus 'two stage' sales. Most mail order items cost less than £50; but if your product costs more, you might find it easier to sell by first sending the customer general information and then actually 'asking' for the sale with a second mailing. The advantage to you is that the first mailing identifies those who are seriously interested, because only they ask for more information. This becomes especially important if you have an expensive brochure, which may have cost as much as £2 per copy to print up. No one can afford to waste that sort of money on people who are only half interested. Through testing you can ascertain whether one or two stage sales are more profitable.

When writing your mailshot, check out the advice given earlier in this chapter for writing the inserts and for copy-writing in general in Chapter 7. The major advantage is that you have unlimited space with which to get across your message; we normally enclose the offer with a covering letter, the whole thing printed on two sides of one sheet. Some people write four-page sales letters. The length and complexity of your message will depend very much upon the nature and price of your product. The more money you are asking for, the longer your message is likely to be. You can go to the trouble of addressing each letter individually, but many people just use 'Dear Reader'.

The covering letter should be short and punchy with any

important words in italics/bold/underlined and the message should move fluently (see opposite). Don't forget to code the response mechanism of the advertisement – otherwise you won't know where the orders came from. This is especially important when you are trying out more than one list at a time. Lastly, you can of course send out the mailshot yourself or alternatively employ a mailing house (see the DMSSB booklet for approved houses).

What response should I expect?

Your response rate will vary from product to product and list to list. The very fastest you could hear from someone would be about five days; two days to get there and an immediate turnaround. I hesitate to suggest what is regarded as a 'normal response'; depending upon the strength of your product this can vary from 0–10 per cent. The standard formula for estimating your eventual result is to double the first 10 days' post. But this is, of course, the wrong place to start your calculations. What you have to do is find out how many items you need to sell to make money. To do this simply divide your total mailing list costs by the profit margin on each item – just as you did to find the break-even point of your newspaper advertising. If your mailing fails to produce at least this number of orders, you are on the wrong track!

The only exception to this rule (as it was for newspaper advertising) is if you have decided to start with a product which only breaks even (or makes a small loss) in the attempt to attract customers who might then buy products with high profit margins. This approach has been tried with great success, for example, with coffee machines that only take a specific (and expensive) brand of coffee. But this method is only recommended when you have more mail order experience and feel fully in control of the financial calculations involved.

If your chosen list is making money, the next step is to 'roll out', i.e. rent and mail out to more names from the same list. At the same time, start sourcing other lists that have a suitable profile.

CARNELL LTD.

Alresford, Nr. Colchester, Essex C07 8AP

Dear Reader

THIS LETTER REVEALS A SIMPLE WAY OF CREATING
£200 A WEEK SPARE-TIME INCOME WORKING FROM HOME!

This may be a time when you and your family could use some EXTRA money. I am not talking about just a few £££s. I am writing to reveal a money-making method that will surprise and delight you, once you put it to work.

In fact, the nearest I can get to describing the EDHAR project is to liken it to a handy little "machine" that "prints fivers"! Of course, that isn't what it is. But the end result is <u>exactly</u> the same, as far as your swelling Bank Balance is concerned. Let me put it another way.

Supposing you <u>could</u> have a "family conference" each week, to decide upon the actual size of the <u>cash sum</u> that you would be able to bank within the next 10-14 days. Suppose also that you could do this <u>each</u> and <u>every</u> week of the year, for so long as you wished! This is the "magic" promise of the EDHAR money-making method, if you care to make use of it.

You'll be assembling a product that has just 3 components, ALL readily obtainable. No skill is needed. Using 2 simple tools which almost every household will own already, each product will be "built" in two minutes. No selling at all is involved! The instant you show this article to friends, neighbours or workmates, the reaction is <u>always</u> the same – "Where can I get one?" and "How much?" At £6.50 each, you'll make "a fiver" a time in almost effortless fashion.

Once you've moved 40 or so a week for a few weeks, you may decide that £200 a week isn't enough extra income. That will be your decision, of course. You may consider assembling <u>one hundred</u> a week, raising your income to an acceptable £500 for <u>less</u> than <u>four</u> hours "work", if you can call it that!

Everything you need to know is crammed into the EDHAR PROJECT MANUAL. Yes, you WILL agree that this slim publication is <u>every</u> bit as good as the "fivers" machine I likened it to. Moreover, I am giving you a cast iron money back guarantee to demonstrate my confidence in this money-spinning idea. You'll find it spelt out at the foot of the advertisement overleaf. But do act promptly if you want that extra £200 a week without delay.

Yours sincerely

Alison Cork
Director

P.S. Money can't buy happiness. But it <u>can</u> bring your family a lifestyle that may have eluded you up to the present time!

Registered in England No. 2470149   VAT Reg. No. 577 4772 287

In essence, renting a mailing list has four main advantages as a means to attract new business:

- The ability to target to a fine degree the individuals most likely to be interested in your product;
- the ability to test prices, headlines and copy freely;
- a greater chance of attracting the customer's attention, with a personalised message sent direct to their home;
- the ability to send a detailed sales message, especially important when offering a higher priced product.

Putting inserts and catalogues in with newsletters, papers and magazines

Many media will accept inserts and catalogues for distribution with their paper/magazine. The rates vary depending upon the media concerned and you should contact the advertising department direct for details. Use *BRAD* to source the media most suitable. The advantage to you is that you can give the reader a full and detailed description of the product being offered, and are not confined to a normal advertisement space; you have plenty of room to get across your message and give the customer plenty of space with the response coupon. The disadvantage is that for cost reasons your print run of inserts is almost bound to be smaller than that of the media covered, so you won't reach the same number of readers you would with an advertisement (in some cases you can stipulate that you want to go into, for example, the northern edition of the paper). You also have no control over the insertion process and have to take it on trust that the job has been done properly.

The cost involved

You may well be able to negotiate the insertion rates, especially if the magazine/paper concerned is relatively new or it is a quiet time of year. You might find an enlightened person who will agree to a per enquiry (PE) deal; an arrangement whereby you bear the cost of printing the insert, the media bear the cost of putting it in with the magazine, then each party takes out their respective costs before splitting all revenues 50/50. Before suggesting this, it is important to make sure you can afford it – remember that you only have half as much revenue with which to make a net profit. On the other hand, you have saved your insertion fees.

Using card decks

Card decks are packs of 20 or so cards, measuring approximately 14 cm × 9 cm, which are sent out either to consumers' home addresses or to businesses. Each card deck is normally based around a theme, e.g. investment, golf and leisure, and sent to those people who have shown a previous interest in that area. Card decks are not normally used to sell products 'off the page', mainly because the card is too small to include all the details plus an acceptable response coupon. Instead they are used to generate leads and enquiries from the consumer which are then followed up with further sales material that hopefully clinches the sale. As with mailing lists, card decks are often used to sell more expensive items. Card decks normally advertise the product on one side and offer a response mechanism on the other (see page 224).

The major advantage of card decks is in their cost. You save substantially by sharing the mailing with other products. For example you pay about £40–50 per 1,000 (1993/4 prices) to take part in a card deck (all print and postage costs inclusive), whereas if you wanted to print and mail out the material on your own, it would cost £180 per 1,000 in postage costs alone! As you can see, the savings are significant. In addition, most companies have a rule that only one of any type of product can go into each card deck, so as to avoid competition.

However, you are committed to a certain volume of cards, normally between 100,000 and 400,000, which forces you to spend £4,000 or more at one time. This could be an insurmountable problem if you are on a very small budget. But if you can afford it, card decks also allow the very valuable option of

Both sides of a card for Rollexa

testing your advertising, by splitting the print run and inserting two different pieces of artwork.

It is impossible to predict your response rate. Your proposition must always be a good one for it to succeed. But the average response is normally just under 1 per cent, with extremes ranging from .01–6 per cent. Don't assume that offering Freepost will necessarily improve your results. It may increase the response, but that response may be poor quality because you have made it so easy to ask for further information. Requesting a stamp usually sorts out the men from the boys!

Of course, everything hinges on the quality of the list, so it is important to research carefully when considering a card deck. Two of the largest operators in this country are ICD and RDP (details at the back of this book).

Card decks are not yet widely used in the UK; we are far surpassed by the USA, who have approximately 800 card deck companies, closely followed by France! In any case, they are an option worth looking into.

Taking part in Post Office mailing schemes

You can also take advantage of special delivery schemes run by the Royal Mail. Household delivery is a service whereby your advertising literature (or any unaddressed mail) is delivered directly to your chosen target homes. As with card decks, only one industry is represented in any one mailing, so you are not fighting with the competition as you might be with a newspaper ad. You can also target the customer quite specifically by:

- selecting either households or households and businesses;
- selection through lifestyle and demographic systems (which classify people and homes). The Acorn system is provided free of charge when you use the household delivery service;
- selecting postcode areas, postcode districts or postcode sectors. Postcode sectors are the smallest unit, allowing you to send out to as few as 2,500 houses at a time (fewer in rural areas).

You are restricted as to the weight and size of your mailing, but not in such a way as to limit the effectiveness of your campaign. There is also a minimum delivery charge of £500 for any one mailing. None the less, this can be a good way to target people at home. Contact details for the household delivery service are at the back of the book.

RENTING OUT YOUR MAILING LIST

Making money from your names

This is a source of revenue which could conceivably bring as much profit as your mainstream activity of display advertising. Moreover, it can be exploited by almost any mail order operator – simply and quickly. You already have the essential raw materials – the names and addresses of people who have bought from you. Now you have to organise this information into one or more saleable lists. Just as you may decide to rent names from other people for mailing purposes, this is your chance to make some money by renting out your own information.

There are five areas to consider when thinking about renting out your mailing list.

Whether to manage the list yourself or have a listbroker handle it for you

If you have fewer than 10,000 names (which will be the case for the first few months at least!), you would do better to handle it yourself. The administration will be minimal and all the rental money remains yours.

This does mean that you will have to purchase a computer and printer if you haven't already done so. The computer will hold the names and addresses of your lists, and the printer will allow you to provide the client with the names printed on to sticky address labels. You also want to be able to offer the customer the option of list selections, i.e. by area, age, product bought etc., and a wordprocessing package is ideal for this. But you need only buy a simple PC and a computer specialist can advise you.

Legal considerations

You will also have to register as a data user with the Data Protection Registrar (see Chapter 6) and observe the data protection principles (so will anyone holding information on their computer on your behalf); perhaps the most important of these is that your list must 'be fairly obtained', i.e. you can only use the names and addresses of people who responded to advertisements which carried an opt-out clause and who didn't subsequently ask to be taken off your list (see Chapter 7). You must withdraw the name and address of any individual who requests it.

You should also become a member of the Mailing Preference Scheme. They will keep you up to date with names of people who do not wish to be sent direct mail; although with only a small list this could prove an expensive service. In addition, your list should have a warranty. This is essentially a promise to your customer and, if relevant, your list broker, that your list has been fairly obtained in accordance with DPR principles. The Direct Marketing Association will send you a sample upon which you can base yours. See the List Owner Warranty overleaf.

How to find your customers

First you have to produce some sales material to get people interested in renting your list. This is referred to as a data card (see page 229) and should ideally give the following information:

- your list profile, i.e. 70 per cent male, recent book purchasers etc.;
- the selections available, i.e. the media source, item bought, date of purchase;
- the cost of renting the list and of printing off labels;
- your terms and conditions, i.e. that the list may only be used once (you can always plant your own dummy names, or 'sleepers', if you want to check against this).

You then have to look for people who are likely to want to rent

LIST OWNER WARRANTY

In respect of rentals of lists supplied to users through

....

IT IS WARRANTED THAT

1.   We are a List Owner as defined.

2.   We are registered as required under the Data Protection Act (1984), registration No....................

3.   Our registration includes PO18 (Trading in personal information) and the disclosures registered under that purpose are compatible with disclosures to List Users. *

4.   The data have been fairly and lawfully obtained, and all the private individuals whose names are included in the lists supplied by us have been given an adequate opportunity to object to the use of any of their data by persons other than ourselves. The names of those who have objected to such use have been:

                                        deleted from the specific list
                                                    or
                                        so marked in the specific list
                                                    or
                        the data have been fairly and lawfully obtained from public sources.

5.   Requests for the correction or deletion of inaccurate data, for the suppression of deceased names or for the marking of disputed data in respect of individuals whose names are included in the lists supplied by us, received either directly or from any other user of the lists have been and will continue to be, complied with no later than 30 days following the receipt of such request by us.

6.   Updating of data in respect of names and addresses included in the lists supplied by us are made no less frequently than every 30 days / ~~90 days / 180 d~~ays. Any changes in this frequency will be notified to users of lists at the time of supply. (Does not apply to lists compiled from public-sources).

7.   Updating of data in respect of most recent transactions by individuals included in the lists supplied by us are made no less frequently than every 30 days / ~~90 days / 180~~ days. Any change in this frequency will be notified to users of lists at the time of supply.

8.   The names of private individuals in the Mailing Preference Service suppression list have been appropriately marked in the rental copies of lists supplied by us no more than 90 days prior to supply.

9.   Lists supplied by us are maintained in accordance with the standards of list and database practice incorporated in the British Code of Advertising Practice. Promotional material despatched to individuals on lists supplied by us must conform with the rules contained in the British Code of Advertising Practice and the British Code of Sales Promotion Practice.

                                        signed..
                                        name..
                                        Company..
                                        Date..

* List Owner definition - means any person with proprietorial rights in any list containing personal data, whether or not he has himself compiled that list and whether or not he is himself a user of that list. The rights referred to include any copyright that may subsist in such a list.

Data Card

Smithco List Rental

10,000 "Cooking for Two" book purchasers. An expanding file. 100% recruited from National Press. All names less than six months old. 100% postcoded and mps cleaned

Selection Information

Males :	3500
Females :	6500
Recency :	✓
Media Source :	✓
Multi buyer :	✓
Date of birth :	X
Geographic	X

List Rental Rates

Base rental charge :	£75 / 1000
Selection costs :	£46 / 1000
Self-Adhesive Labels :	£6 / 1000
Delivery (48 hours) :	£20 / 1000

Terms

Owners approval sample required
One time usage only
Minimum order 4,000 names

Smithco, 27 Jones St, London SW2 1AP Tel: 071 5555555
                                        Fax: 071 6666666

Compiling information for list rental customers

your list. A good place to start is the Sunday colour supplement sections. See who is selling products related to yours (beware of renting to competitors!) and approach them direct. Alternatively, place a small classified ad in trade magazines such as *Direct Response*, *Precision Marketing* and *Direct Mail International*. You shouldn't have too much trouble attracting customers, especially if your list is strong; people are always on the lookout for new names. After a while people will start coming to you.

What to charge
Most good lists cost between £70 and £100/1,000 to rent (1993/4 prices). Recency, i.e. if the names are less than a year old, adds value to a list. You can also charge a premium to anyone using the list for the first time because the names are fresh. You should be quite safe if you follow the prices asked by list brokers for similar lists. In addition, you will have to charge the client approx £6/1,000 for sticky labels and £4/1,000 for cheshire labels (sticky labels designed to be fed into a laser printer rather than a dot matrix printer).

Always insist upon the money up front
Don't send out the names until you have banked the cheque. This is normal procedure in the list rental business, simply because if someone doesn't have much luck with your list, they may just decide not to pay you!

What a listbroker can do for you and how much they will charge
If your list is sizeable (over 10,000 names), you might do well to hand it to a list broker. The advantage to you is that they may be able to rent the lists more frequently by making use of their extensive client base and contacts. They are also relieving you of a workload. The disadvantages are that your list may not be noticed among the hundreds of others on offer and, also, that the list broker will take a fee of about 20 per cent of all your rental income. None the less, if you just want some extra money

for very little effort, a list broker may be the answer. The only way to choose which one to go with is to meet up with a few, ask how they intend to market the list and select the one you feel most comfortable with. You are perfectly entitled to place your lists with more than one broker at a time.

Lastly, don't forget that it actually costs you very little to generate revenue from list rental. Most of the income goes straight to your bottom line as profit, so do take advantage of this little money-making machine. It is one of the great 'perks' of mail order!

CONCLUSION

T HE WORLD OF MAIL ORDER is fascinating, fun and full of opportunities. It is also 'democratic' – anyone with a good product to sell has the potential to make money, regardless of their background and experience. At its simplest level, you could set up with just a desk and a telephone in the back room at home. Moreover, you could trade nationwide from that desk. Mail order is also flexible. You can decide to make just a bit of extra pocket money, or aim for big business and the really serious profit. Most important, you can impose a strict limit on the financial risk involved.

Mail order has undoubtedly come of age, particularly in the UK. Increasing numbers of people are turning to the convenience of postal buying and, equally, more people want to work from home – a situation ideally suited to mail order. Flexibility, independence, a better lifestyle, motherhood and sadly, redundancy, are just a few of the reasons why mail order has become an expanding field for the homeworker. In addition, more and more companies are discovering that mail order is one of the simplest, most cost-effective ways of expanding their operation, offering a whole new profit centre to be exploited with minimum start-up costs and disruption. There has never been a better time to join in. Having read this book, you now have the information necessary to do just that.

Mail order could conceivably change your life, so think of this as the first day of your mail order 'career'. Follow the principles in this book, remember to be cautious and, above all, concentrate on the results of your advertisements. All the answers to your mail order business will lie in those files. I wish you all the luck in the world. So go out there and run a tight ship. I wish you the very best of luck.

ALISON CORK
June 1993

GLOSSARY

Body copy The main text of an advertisement.

Bounce back Or 'back end' – both terms are used to describe the sales made to a customer subsequent to their first purchase.

Bromide A photographic image of a piece of artwork.

Cash flow Flows of cash going into and out from a business, and in particular, the difference between them.

Column size The width of the columns in individual newspapers and magazines.

Database Information, usually names and addresses, kept as a computer file.

Dead time Time that is not being used to make money.

Dealing Negotiating, usually advertising rates.

Fractional ad An advertisement which takes up only part of a page.

Fulfilment Receiving, processing and dispatching customer orders.

Gross profit Your profit before you charge overheads.

Mailing list List of names and addresses of people with particular characteristics in common.

Mailshot The advertising material sent out to the names and addresses on a mailing list.

Media amendment report Confirmation of advertisements booked on your behalf by an agency/media buyer.

Media buyer Someone whose job it is to purchase advertising space on behalf of a client.

Operating profit Your gross profit minus overheads.

Opt-out clause A clause, usually at the bottom of an advertisement, which allows the customer to inform the advertiser whether or not they wish to receive further mailings.

Point size The height by which type is measured.

Roll out Extending an advertising campaign.

Solus position When there is only one advertisement on a particular page.

Space Advertising space.

Typesetting Means by which text or copy is prepared for printing.

Uplift Increase in response.

SUGGESTED READING

Advertising That Pulls Response by Graeme McCorkell (McGraw-Hill).

Be Your Own PR Expert by Bill Penn (Piatkus).

The British Code of Advertising Practice (free from the ASA).

Common Sense Direct Marketing by Drayton Bird (Kogan Page).

The Craft of Copywriting by Alastair Crompton (Business Books Ltd).

The Daily Mail Book of Running a Small Business and Working from Home by Jennie Hawthorne (Harmony Books).

Do Your Own Advertising by Alastair Crompton (Business Books Ltd).

Glossary of Direct Marketing Terms (DMA).

How To Keep Business Accounts by Peter Taylor (Northcote House Publishers Ltd).

How to Start a Business From Home by Graham Jones (Northcote House Publishers Ltd).

Making Money From Your Garden by Barty Phillips (Piatkus).

The Secrets of Effective Direct Mail by John Frazer Robinson (McGraw-Hill).

Selling by Direct Mail by John W. Graham and Susan K. Jones (Piatkus).

Successful Marketing for Small Businesses by Nigel Hill (The Royal Bank of Scotland in conjunction with Charles Letts and Co.)

Understand Your Accounts by A. St J. Price (Kogan Page Ltd).

USEFUL
ADDRESSES

Advertising Standards Authority and Committee of Advertising
Practice, Brook House, 2–16 Torrington Place, London WC1E 7HN
Tel: 071–580 5555.

Advertising Standards Authority for Ireland, IPC House,
35–39 Shelbourne Road, Dublin 4.
Tel: 010 353 16 608 766.   Fax: 010 353 16 608 113.

Association of Media Independents, 48 Percy Road, London
N12 8BU.
Tel: 081–343 7779.   Fax: 081–446 6794.

BRAD (all versions of), Maclean Hunter Ltd, Maclean Hunter
House, Chalk Lane, Cockfosters Road, Barnet, Herts. EN4 0BU
Tel: 081–975 9759.   Fax: 081–440 9930
BRAD is also the sole UK subscription agent for the media guides
serving: Canada, Belgium, France, Germany, Italy, Spain,
Scandinavia, Austria, Switzerland, The Netherlands, China, the
Middle East, South Africa and Australia.

Chartered Association of Certified Accountants, 29 Lincoln's Inn
Fields, London WC2A 3EE.
Tel: 071–242 6855.   Fax: 071–831 8054.

Data Protection Registrar, Westcliffe House, Water Lane,
Wilmslow, Cheshire, SK9 5AX.
Tel: 0625 535777.   Fax: 0625 524510.

Direct Mail Information Service, housed by the HBH Partnership, 5 Carlisle Street, London W1V 5RG.
Tel: 071–494 0483.   Fax: 071–494 0455.

Direct Mail Services Standards Board, 26 Eccleston Street, London SW1W 9PY.
Tel: 071–824 8651.   Fax: 071–824 8574.

The Direct Marketing Association (UK) Limited, Haymarket House, 1 Oxendon Street, London SW1Y 4EE.
Tel: 071–321 2525.   Fax: 071–321 0191.

Direct Selling Association, 29 Floral Street, London WC2E 9DP.
Tel: 071–497 1234.   Fax: 071–497 3144.

Dudley Jenkins Group PLC, 2a Southwark Bridge Office Village, Thrale Street, London SE1 9JG.
Tel: 071–407 4753.   Fax: 071–407 6294.

Exhibition Industry Federation, PO Box 980, London SE11 5JB.
Tel: 071–582 6899.   Fax: 071–793 0293.

Home Business, Merlin Publications, 14 Hove Business Centre, Fonthill Road, Hove BN3 6HA.
Tel: 0273 888992.   Fax: 0273 888994.

Home Run, published by Sophie Chalmers, Active Information, 79 Black Lion Lane, London W6 9BG.
Tel: 081–846 9244.

ICD, 91–93 Charter House Street, London EC1M 6HR.
Tel: 071–251 2883.

Incorporated Society of British Advertisers, 44 Hertford Street, London W1Y 8AE.
Tel: 071–499 7502.   Fax: 071–629 5355.

Inland Revenue (see your local telephone directory).

Institute of Chartered Accountants in England and Wales,
PO Box 433, Chartered Accountants' Hall, Moorgate Place,
London EC2P 2BJ.
Tel: 071–920 8100.   Fax: 071–920 0547.

Institute of Chartered Accountants in Ireland, Chartered
Accountants House, 87–89 Pembroke Road, Dublin 4.
Tel: 010 353 16 680 400.   Fax: 010 353 16 680 842.

Institute of Chartered Accountants of Scotland, 27 Queen Street,
Edinburgh, EH2 1LA.
Tel: 031–225 5673.   Fax: 031–225 3813.

Kompass, Reed Information Services Ltd, Windsor Court, East
Grinstead, West Sussex RH19 1XD.
Tel: 0342 335861.   Fax: 0342 335992.

The List and Database Suppliers Group (contactable through the
DMSSB).

Mailing Preference Service, 1 Leeward House, Square Rigger Row,
Plantation Wharf, Battersea, London SW11 3TY.
Tel: 071–738 1625.

Mail Order Protection Scheme (for national daily newspapers),
16 Took's Court, London EC4A 1LB.
Tel: 071–405 6806.   Fax: 071–404 0106.

Mail Order Traders' Association (for catalogue mail order) 100 Old
Hall Street, Liverpool, L3 9TD.
Tel: 051–227 4181.

Mail Users' Association, 3 Pavement House, The Pavement, Hay
on Wye, Hereford and Worcester HR3 3BU.
Tel: 0497 821357.   Fax: 0497 821360.

Mardev Ltd, 151–153 Wardour Street, London W1V 3TB.
Tel: 071–411 2666.   Fax: 071–287 1098.

Mintel International Group Ltd, 18–19 Long Lane, London EC1A 9HE.
Tel: 071–606 6000.   Fax: 071–606 5932.

The Newspaper Society (for regional and local newspapers), 74–77 Great Russell Street, London WC1B 3DA.
Tel: 071–636 7014.   Fax: 071–631 5119.

Office of Fair Trading, Field House, Bream's Buildings, London EC4A 1PR.
Tel: 071–242 2858.

Periodical Publishers' Association Ltd (for magazines), Imperial House, 15–19 Kingsway, London WC2B 6UN.
Tel: 071–379 6268.   Fax: 071–379 5661.

Provincial Newspapers Association of Ireland, 33 Parkgate Street, Dublin 8.
Tel: 010 353 16 793 679.

RDP, Verney House, 1b Hollywood Road, London SW10 9HS.
Tel: 071–351 3535.

Reuben Ash Ltd, 3 Tribune Avenue, Hanover Business Park, Broadheath, Altrincham, Cheshire.
Tel/Fax: 061–929 5393.

Richard Joseph Publishers Ltd, Unit 1 & 2, Monks Walk, Farnham, Surrey GU9 8HT.
Tel: 0252 734347.

Royal Mail Streamline, PO Box 1000, Oxford OX4 5XA.
Tel: 0865 780400.
Handles Household Delivery Service, Mailsort, Response Services and Packet Post.

The Scottish Daily Newspaper Society (for Scottish daily newspapers), 30 George Square, Glasgow G2 1EG.
Tel: 041–248 2375.

Scottish Newspaper Publishers' Association (for Scottish regional and local newspapers), 48 Palmerston Place, Edinburgh EH12 5DE.
Tel: 031–220 4353.   Fax: 031–220 4344.

Sherelle International Ltd, 20–26 College Street, Southampton SO9 5AD.
Tel: 0703 221957.

Tolson Messenger Ltd, 148 King Street, London W6 0QU.
Tel: 081–741 8361.   Fax: 081–741 9395.
Insurance broker which offers specially designed policies for people working from home.

Trading Standards Office (contact your local council for details).

Verified Free Distribution Ltd, Black Prince Yard, 207 High Street, Berkhamstead, Herts HP4 1AD.
Tel: 0442 863344.   Fax: 0442 877409.

INDEX

Piatkus Business Books

Piatkus Business Books have been created for people who need expert knowledge readily available in a clear and easy-to-follow format. All the books are written by specialists in their field. They will help you improve your skills quickly and effortlessly in the workplace and on a personal level. Titles include:

General Management and Business Skills

Beware the Naked Man Who Offers You His Shirt Harvey Mackay

Be Your Own PR Expert: the complete guide to publicity and public relations Bill Penn

Brain Power: the 12-week mental training programme Marilyn vos Savant and Leonore Fleischer

Complete Conference Organiser's Handbook, The Robin O'Connor

Complete Time Management System, The Christian H Godefroy and John Clark

Confident Decision Making J Edward Russo and Paul J H Schoemaker

Creating Abundance Andrew Ferguson

Creative Thinking Michael LeBoeuf

Dealing with Difficult People Roberta Cava

Energy Factor, The: how to motivate your workforce Art McNeil

Firing On All Cylinders: the quality management system for high-powered corporate performance Jim Clemmer with Barry Sheehy

Great Boom Ahead, The Harry Dent

How to Choose Stockmarket Winners Raymond Caley

How to Implement Corporate Change John Spencer and Adrian Pruss

How to Run a Part-Time Business Barrie Hawkins

Influential Manager, The: how to develop a powerful management style Lee Bryce

Leadership Skills for Every Manager Jim Clemmer and Art McNeil

Lure the Tiger Out of the Mountains: timeless tactics from the East for today's successful manager Gao Yuan

Managing Your Team John Spencer and Adrian Pruss

Memory Booster: easy techniques for rapid learning and a better memory Robert W Finkel

Perfectly Legal Tax Loopholes Stephen Courtney

Play to Your Strengths Donald O Clifton and Paula Nelson

Problem Employees: how to improve their behaviour and their performance Peter Wylie and Mardy Grothe

Problem Solving Techniques That Really Work Malcolm Bird

Psychological Testing for Managers Dr Stephanie Jones

Quantum Learning: unleash the genius within you Bobbi DePorter with Mike Hernacki

Right Brain Manager, The: how to use the power of your mind to achieve personal and professional success Dr Harry Alder

Seven Cultures of Capitalism, The: value systems for creating wealth in Britain, the United States, Germany, France, Japan, Sweden and the Netherlands Charles Hampden-Turner and Fons Trompenaars

Sharkproof: get the job you want, keep the job you love in today's tough job market Harvey Mackay

Smart Questions for Successful Managers Dorothy Leeds

10-Day MBA, The Steven Silbiger

Sales and Customer Services
Art of the Hard Sell, The Robert L Shook

Creating Customers David H Bangs

Guerrilla Marketing Excellence Jay Conrad Levinson

How to Close Every Sale Joe Girard

How to Collect the Money You Are Owed Malcolm Bird

How to Succeed in Network Marketing

How to Win Customers and Keep Them for Life Michael LeBoeuf

Making Profits: a six-month plan for the small business Malcolm Bird

Sales Power: The Silva mind method for sales professionals José Silva and Ed Bernd Jr

Selling Edge, The Patrick Forsyth

Telephone Selling Techniques That Really Work Bill Good

Winning Edge, The Charles Templeton

Winning New Business: a practical guide to successful sales presentations Dr David Lewis

Presentation and Communication
Better Business Writing Maryann V Piotrowski

Complete Book of Business Etiquette, The Lynne Brennan and David Block

Outstanding Negotiator, The Christian H Godefroy and Luis Robert

Personal Power Philippa Davies

For a free brochure with further information on our complete range of business titles, please write to:

Piatkus Books
Freepost 7 (WD 4505)
London W1E 4EZ

PIATKUS